How to
Find, Follow, Fulfill

by

Andrew Wommack

Harrison House
Tulsa, OK

21   8

How to Find, Follow, Fulfill

ISBN: 978-160683-506-7

Copyright © 2013 by Andrew Wommack

Colorado Springs, CO 80907

Published by:

Harrison House Publishers, LLC

Tulsa, OK 7414

Table of Contents

Chapter One

God Created You for a Purpose

Recently I was teaching at a Bible college about God's will and asked the question, "How many of you aren't sure you're doing what God created you for?" I said, "You may want it, you may desire it, you may be praying that God will take all of the things you do and use them to further His kingdom, but how many of you aren't certain that you're doing what God created you to do?" Over half of the people in the room raised their hands to say they weren't positive they were doing what God called them to do—and those were fanatics who came out on a Thursday morning just to hear the Gospel!

You are not going to accidentally fulfill God's will. It doesn't happen unintentionally or by coincidence. Seeing God's will realized in your life means, first of all, finding out what unique purpose He created you for. In nature, water always seeks the path of least resistance and our human nature does the same thing if we allow it to. We can end up meandering through life, allowing obstacles we encounter to determine what direction we take. But it doesn't have to be that way. God intends for us to experience the satisfaction of a life well lived. We can do this if we are willing to do more than just go with the flow—even a dead fish can float downstream.

Accomplishing the things we were created to achieve means making a deliberate effort to find, follow, and fulfill God's will. When I put forth effort to discover my God-given purpose, it was a critical turning point in my life. I was in high school at the time and until then everything had been decided for me. But as I approached the end of my senior year, I realized I was going to have to start making some decisions on my own. This brought me face to face with the question we all eventually ask: *What is the purpose for my life?*

One thing I am grateful that I learned while growing up in church is that God created everyone with a purpose. Your parents may not have known you were coming, but God did. God created you. You didn't evolve. You aren't a mistake. God created you, and He created you for a reason.

As I wrestled with what to do about my future, I knew that God had a purpose for my life, so I didn't want to just randomly pick a direction. I began asking people in my church, "How do you know God's will for your life? How do you find it?" Unfortunately, nobody could tell me. I didn't know of any method for discovering God's will, so I started studying the Word of God. I knew that the Bible contained knowledge about God, so I figured it was a good place to look for God's will for my life. I began to stay up until two or three o'clock every morning studying the Bible.

I had read the Bible every day of my life since I was a little kid, but I never really studied it, so I went out and bought a Bible commentary to help me understand everything. I had about five volumes of these big old heavy books, and I would sit there and study every single verse. I remember using a lamp with a flexible goose neck that allowed me to position it in different ways. I used to pull the lamp down over my Bible and read with my head perched above the lamp casing. Whenever I started to fall asleep, my forehead would nod down onto the lamp and it would burn me, jarring me back awake so I would keep on reading. That was how I forced myself to stay up and read the Bible.

Although I read through the entire Bible two or three times that year, I didn't feel like God had shown me anything special. I didn't receive any specific revelations. I was just preparing the ground. Before planting a seed, you have to dig out the rocks and prepare the ground so the seed can sink in. That's what I was doing; I was seeking the Lord. I did that for over a year, and then, all of a sudden, something opened up.

I beseech you therefore, brethren, by the mercies of God, that ye present your bodies a living sacrifice, holy, acceptable unto God, which is your reasonable service. And be not conformed to this world: but be ye transformed by the renewing of your mind, that ye may prove what is that good, and acceptable, and perfect, will of God.

Romans 12:1-2

This passage of scripture came alive to me. It burned in my heart. I spent months reading it and asking God, "What does this mean? How do I do it?" Then some time later, I had a miraculous encounter with the Lord and experienced His love for me. It turned my life upside down and for more than four months, I was caught up in the presence of God. It changed me.

Often when I talk about this miraculous encounter with God, people think that it was a fluke—like lightning or something. They think, "You never know where it's going to strike." Actually, I've heard that lightning doesn't come from the sky down. It looks that way, but there is a negative charge in the ground that attracts the lightning—so it really starts *in* the ground. You can see this in time-lapse photos of a lightning strike. The reality is that lightning strikes certain places for a reason.

Likewise, there are reasons why God all of a sudden captures one person's life with a miraculous encounter, while others don't encounter Him at all. It's true that you can't make God reveal something to you by saying, "God, tell me what I want to know, right now." It doesn't work like that. But you can prepare your heart.

In my situation, I didn't really understand what was happening in me. I wasn't mature enough to know what was going on—I was just hungry for God. I wanted to know God's purpose for my life. I had been seeking Him in the best way I knew how to for 18 months. It wasn't an accident that God showed up. I knew He had a purpose for me and my life was turned around when I became hungry to discover it. As a result of my hunger, God touched me, and I've never gotten over it. It changed my life!

A popular misconception in the church today is that God winds us up like a doll and then lets us go our own way, leaving us to figure life out on our own. "If I get in a bind," the thinking goes, "I can call on God and *maybe* He'll help me." This kind of philosophy leads people to do their own thing in life and then ask God to bless what they are already doing—instead of seeking Him for direction from the beginning.

Since I found God's will for my life, I don't ever pray for God to bless what I'm doing. I don't even pray for the meetings I hold around the country, which shocks some people. I have been asked, "You didn't spend time praying and interceding before the meeting?" No, because God told me to hold those meetings. He would be unjust to command me to do something and then expect me to do it in my own strength and power. God gives me an anointing to do what He has called me to do. It's the same for everyone. When you are doing what God called you to do, you don't have to spend time asking for His blessing or praying for Him to move on your behalf. God has already blessed what He told you to do.

One reason so many people are praying for God to come to their assistance is because they aren't doing what He told them to do. Others may have stumbled into God's will for their life, but they don't have that assurance and joy that comes from knowing they are exactly where He wants them to be.

Is Someone Waiting on You?

I believe there is a supernatural peace that goes along with being in the center of God's will. Something changes in you when you know you are where God wants you to be. I remember an encounter I had in Charlotte, North Carolina, where I have ministered every year since the 1980s. A friend of mine has a business there and invites me to come speak to his employees. One year I spoke at his business and as I was leaving, I saw an Asian woman answering the phones. I had never seen her before, so I stopped and started talking to her.

"Are you new here?" I asked.

"Yes," she said, "I just started last week."

"Oh, okay. Well, how come you weren't back there with the rest of the employees?"

"I'm the new person, so they had me answer the phone," she answered. "Who are you?"

I told her who I was, and she said, "What do you do?"

"I'm a minister."

"For whom?" she asked.

"For Jesus." I said.

"You must be the one!" she exclaimed.

I asked her what she was talking about and she explained that she was a Buddhist. The night before, she had been performing her Buddhist worship and was suddenly disillusioned with the whole thing and said, "This isn't it. Buddha is not it." She told me how she spoke out, "God I know *You* are real. I know You exist, but I don't know who You are. Would you reveal Yourself to me?" Then she recounted how a pulsating ball of light appeared and hung right in front of her. She said she knew it was God, but she asked anyway, "Who are You?" A voice replied, "Tomorrow, I'll send you a man who will tell you who I am."

"You must be the one," she exclaimed again.

"I'm the one," I said.

I went on to tell her about Jesus and she was born again and baptized in the Holy Spirit. It was awesome! I left that place thinking, *God, I was in the right place at the right time!* I was exactly where I was supposed to be. God knew He could count on me to be there and to follow His leading, so He told that woman to expect me. I can't even describe the peace, satisfaction, and joy that comes from knowing you are right where God wants you to be. If that doesn't make you have a good day, nothing will. Something happens when you know that everything about you is doing what God created you to do.

Many people have never felt the satisfaction of knowing, beyond the shadow of a doubt, that they are doing what God made them for. No believer should live that way. God created you for something better than wandering aimlessly through life. You have a purpose.

A Holy Dissatisfaction

The only way to have perfect peace and joy is to point your life in the direction God wants you to go. Otherwise, you may be praying to get rid of discouragement in your life when, in fact, the lack of peace you are experiencing is a result of not being in God's perfect will. When you aren't going in the right direction, He will sometimes turn you around by giving you a sense of unrest, or what I call a "holy dissatisfaction."

We need to understand that the "holy dissatisfaction" that comes from God is totally different from depression. The depression that comes from the world is a result of giving your attention to the flesh, instead of focusing on the things of God (Romans 8:6). The dissatisfaction that God uses to give direction to believers who are seeking Him is completely different from the turmoil of negative emotions. God doesn't use depression to guide us.

When my wife, Jamie, and I pastored a church in Seagoville, Texas, there were times when friends tried to talk us into leaving. They would say, "People aren't receiving the message, nobody wants you, just move on." It was true, people stayed away from our church by the droves. But we were committed to Seagoville, Texas. We loved the people and were happy; so we stayed there and kept on ministering.

Everything was great until one day when I was in church praying—it was like somebody flipped a switch on the inside of me. All of a sudden, I looked out the window over the town and thought, *God, what am I doing here? If this isn't the end of the world, you can see it from here.* The desires of my heart changed in an instant and suddenly I hated being in Seagoville.

This change in how I felt was so abrupt that it kind of surprised me. It was only the day before that I was happy and excited about simply having the opportunity to minister there. Then, without any apparent reason, I didn't want to be in Seagoville anymore. I started praying and seeking God for clarity and within an hour or two I was convinced that God was telling me to leave. In fact, He even gave me a date. He told me that we would be leaving our house by the first of November. I was sure of it, so I started toward home wondering how I was going to tell Jamie that we were moving. When I arrived home, there was already a "For Sale" sign in our front yard!

I walked into the house and asked Jamie, "What is that sign doing in the yard?" She said, "The landlord came by and said we have to be out November first."

God didn't give me direction by a booming voice that echoed down from the heavens saying, "*Thus saith the Lord, thou shalt leave Seagoville, Texas.*" No, I just lost my desire to be there. This is one of the ways that God speaks to us—through the desires of our heart.

One of the reasons that some people aren't satisfied with getting up and going to work, coming home, watching television, going to bed, and then getting up and doing the whole thing over again, is because they aren't doing what God called them to do. It's a holy dissatisfaction. You are never going to have the sense of joy and peace that I've been talking about until you get in line with God's will for your life. Unless you are doing what God created you to do, you will never have the drive that continually wakes you up in the morning excited about life, knowing that you are on a path that is making a difference and changing others.

It's sad to say, but a lot of Christians have never known the satisfaction that comes from being in the center of God's will. One of the reasons for this is because the church has been more *influenced* by the world rather than *influencing* the world.

Many of us were raised, whether in a Christian home or not, to think that our life is our own and we can do whatever we want with it. Still, others grew up thinking they were a mistake because their parents told them they were the result of an unplanned pregnancy. Some look around and feel like they missed out on the talents and abilities they see in others. In one way or another, many people go through life feeling like they are a mistake—so they just struggle and try to cope the best they can.

The Lord's plan for your life is far better than that. You aren't a mistake. You didn't miss out on the talents you need to accomplish God's will. You don't have to struggle through life, bouncing from one crisis to the next. God has a purpose for you. He created you for a reason. You have a specific purpose in life and God wants you to discover that purpose.

Separated from the Womb

I praise You because I am fearfully and wonderfully made;
Your works are wonderful,
I know that full well.
My frame was not hidden from You
when I was made in the secret place.
When I was woven together in the depths of the earth,
Your eyes saw my unformed body.
All the days ordained for me
were written in Your book before one of them came to be.
How precious to me are Your thoughts, O God!
How vast is the sum of them!

Psalm 139:14-17 NIV

What a tremendous passage of scripture! God saw you before you were ever born. He saw you in your mother's womb. At the same time you were being physically formed, God wove in your talents, abilities, and purpose. It's a part of who you are. Before you were even born, God had already written down what your life is supposed to be. He had written down your talents and abilities.

You may think you made yourself an artist, or an accountant, or whatever it is that you are, but you can't bring out what God didn't put in. God gave you a disposition. He gave you a certain inclination. Some people are vivacious and lively, while others are quiet and reserved. God gave you the personality you have. He made you the way you are. You can change to a degree, but you can't change the core of who you are.

I used to be a runner but now I'm a walker. In high school, they tried to make me run sprints—50 yard dashes. I did it, but I hated it and was never really good at it. I was good enough to make the track team, but never good enough to win any medals. After I finished school, I started jogging and discovered that I loved to jog. I enjoyed running 15 or 20 miles slowly, but running 50 yards as fast as I could really bothered me.

I eventually learned that muscles are made up of fast-twitch and slow-twitch fibers. Sprinters have a majority of fast-twitch muscle fibers, while distance runners have more slow-twitch muscle fibers. You can change the ratio of fast-twitch to slow-twitch fibers in your muscles through training, but not by much. The basic balance doesn't change. Some people are built for speed; others are built for endurance. I didn't like sprinting because I wasn't built to run sprints. I was built for long-distance running.

In the same way, your personality can be influenced and changed to a degree, but you have a genetic disposition to be a certain type of person with a certain type of personality. You were designed that way. Before you were formed, God had already planned those things. He had it written out. He wove in your abilities and purpose, but He won't force His will for your life to come to pass. This is something that keeps people from recognizing and finding God's will for their lives. They have a fatalistic attitude that whatever is meant to be, will be—like that old song, "Qué será, será. Whatever will be, will be."

If you let fate dictate your life, you will make a lot of wrong decisions. You can't just let circumstances move and control you. God doesn't move you around like a pawn. Many think God is sovereign and whatever His will is comes to pass, but that isn't how it works.

God is sovereign, in the sense that He has supreme power and is Master of all things, seen and unseen. But He is not sovereign in the sense that nothing can happen without His permission. God doesn't control your life. He doesn't force His will to come to pass. Everything that happens in your life is not God's will. I know a lot of people teach that nothing can happen unless God wills it to happen, but that isn't what the Word of God says. For example, the Apostle Peter wrote:

> *The Lord is not slack concerning his promise, as some men count slackness; but is longsuffering to us-ward, not willing that any should perish, but that all should come to repentance.*

> *2 Peter 3:9*

It's very clear that God doesn't want anyone to miss out on salvation. He desires for everyone to receive salvation, yet Jesus said there would be more people who perish by entering the broad gate that leads to destruction than those who are saved by entering through the narrow gate that leads to everlasting life (Matthew 7:13-14). God wants every person to be saved, yet not everyone will be saved. Jesus even prophesied that not everyone will be saved.

The reason God's will does not automatically come to pass in our lives is that we have a part to play. We choose whether or not we will be saved by our response to Jesus. We have a choice in the matter. In the same way, God has a plan for you but you have control over your own life. God is not going to make His will come to pass in your life without your cooperation.

Before you were born, before you were even formed in the womb, God had a plan for your life. You were born a man or a woman, at this time in history, in the nation you were born in for a reason. It isn't a coincidence. God chose you. He has a purpose for you and He gave you gifts and abilities to accomplish that purpose. God created you for a reason and has a specific plan for what He wants you to do, but ultimately *you* are in control.

Steps and Stages

If you feel like a square peg in a round hole, it might be because you have allowed circumstances to move you away from the direction God has planned for you. The reason you aren't satisfied or fulfilled is that you aren't moving in the right direction. You will never have the degree of success you could have in life until you find God's will.

When I first started seeking the Lord, I knew I was called to minister but I didn't know in what capacity. Over a period of time, I discovered that I was called to teach, as opposed to being an evangelist. My gifting was toward the body of Christ, to help believers learn who they are in Christ. Initially, however, I didn't know exactly what area of ministry I was called to so I started out by holding Bible studies. This was back before there was such a thing as a Spirit-filled church. People thought that if you spoke in tongues, you were of the devil. I actually made a top 10 list of things that were "of the devil" in my town—I was number one on the list!

All of the people who came to my Bible studies were kicked out of their churches, so they said, "We're going to start tithing here. This is our church now."

"Wait a second," I told them. "This isn't a church, it's a Bible study. And I'm not a pastor."

"Well, you can call it whatever you want to," they said, "but we don't have anywhere else to go. This is where we go, so you're our pastor."

I became a pastor by default. I didn't want to be a pastor. I never felt called to be a pastor. But the people in my Bible study started calling me "Pastor," and I ended up pastoring three churches. God used me in that role: lives were changed, people were born again, and good things happened, but it wasn't my calling.

After I started on radio, I held my first Gospel meeting when I advertised the event during my broadcast and invited everyone who could make it to come out. It was awesome! After the very first meeting, I knew that I was made to travel and minister in exactly that way. Even though I had been teaching the same things before, I felt a new sense of liberty, satisfaction, and joy when I started ministering in the way God created me to.

I wasn't out of His will when I was pastoring those three churches, it was a time of training for me. God taught me during that period and I learned a lot, but I wasn't yet in the *center* of His will. You don't go from *not* being in God's will to instantly being in the center of His will. It's a process. It takes time; it happens progressively.

I started ministering in 1968. On July 26, 1999, the Lord woke me up in the middle of the night and spoke to me about some things. He told me I was just then beginning to fulfill what He had called me to do and if I had died before then, I would have missed His perfect will for my life. It was both discouraging and encouraging at the same time to hear those things.

It was discouraging because I had been ministering for 31 years and saw great things happen, but the Lord was telling me that I was just then getting to the center of His will. But it also encouraged me, because I was already seeing God do wonderful things and felt extremely blessed to be doing what He had called me to do. I thought, *If I'm just now getting closer to doing what God called me to do, then it's going to get even better!* And it has. Our ministry has grown extensively and we're reaching more people than ever with the Gospel. I have to run to keep up. It's awesome! But we didn't get here overnight.

The reason you might find life hard or might not be experiencing satisfaction is because God created you to do something different from what you are doing. He created you for one thing and you are off doing something else. Maybe you just fell into what you are doing; you were recruited at a college career day or got married and took whatever opportunity you could. Life might have just kind of taken a path on its own, which happens. I hope you recognize now that God created you for a unique purpose and you have to intentionally pursue that purpose.

God Is Not Looking at Your Resume

For ye have heard of my conversation in time past in the Jews' religion, how that beyond measure I persecuted the church of God, and wasted it: And profited in the Jews' religion above many my equals in mine own nation, being more exceedingly zealous of the traditions of my fathers. But when it pleased God, who separated me from my mother's womb, and called me by His grace…

Galatians 1:13-15

When the Apostle Paul wrote that God had *separated* him, he meant that God had set him apart for a specific purpose. God set Paul apart from his mother's womb to preach the Gospel. This is a radical thought. We always look at a person's qualifications when we are trying to fill a position in church or in the workplace. We want to know if the applicant is reliable. We look at their accomplishments and natural abilities, and essentially choose people based on their past performance. But God's way is different.

This passage of Scripture says that God chose Paul and set him apart from his mother's womb to preach the Gospel—before he ever did anything good or bad or developed his talents and abilities. God isn't looking at your resume and saying, "Oh, look at what you've accomplished. You would be a great choice. I think I'll call you to do such and such." No, God doesn't work like that. From the very moment of conception, God had a plan, and from your mother's womb, God already had a purpose designed for you.

Our talents and abilities can be an indication of God's will, but many of us have hidden talents and gifts that we have never recognized or developed. If we only look at what we *think* our talents and abilities are, we will miss God. We won't see our real potential until we get beyond ourselves and get into a realm of trusting God for something supernatural. We can't just say, "Well, I've always been able to speak in front of people, so maybe God wants me to be a preacher, or something like that." We aren't going to find God's will that way.

I used to be someone who couldn't look other people in the face and speak to them. I remember walking down the street one day when I was a senior in high school and a man walked past me and said, "Good morning." He was two blocks down the street before I let out my response, "Good morning, sir."

I got into my car and sat there thinking, "*God, what is wrong with me?*" I was so introverted. Looking at my natural qualifications up to that point, the last thing you would think I would ever end up doing is speaking in front of thousands of people. But God has called me to do something totally contrary to my nature.

God has changed me, but I still like being alone. I really enjoy it. When I want to have a great time, I'll go spend some time by myself—that's my nature. God called me to do something oppo-site from my natural inclination. Too many people are trying to figure out what to do with their lives by looking at their natural abilities, or worse, looking at the results of a personality test. A test can't tell you what God's plan for your life is. A personality test can give you a snapshot of where you are at the time you take the test, but the results aren't true forever.

If I would have taken a personality test before God touched me in 1968, I guarantee you I would have tested as an extreme introvert. But if I took that same test today, I'd test out a maximum extrovert. A test is just a snapshot of where you are. It may tell you what your personality type is like at that moment, but it can't tell you God's real plan and purpose for your life. Some people have been so wounded and beaten into submission by life that the snap-shot isn't going to give them a true indication of their potential.

God didn't look at Paul when he was 20 or 30 years old and say, "Wow, you've spent 20 years studying under Gamaliel and have all of this knowledge under your belt, so I think I'll use you to preach the Gospel and write half the New Testament." God doesn't operate that way. As a matter of fact, most of us would have picked Peter to go to the heathen believing he was half heathen himself. When Jesus called Peter, he was probably out there in the boat cussing. Peter had an attitude. It seemed like the only time he opened his mouth was to change feet! He was always doing something wrong.

Peter wasn't polished or religious, so most of us would have thought he would have been a great guy to send to the heathen—and we would have sent Paul to the Jews! Paul was schooled in the Jewish religion; he knew the law frontward and backward. He also had a revelation of grace. Who better to convince a legalistic Jew than Paul? He was the greatest Pharisee of them all. Yet, God sent Paul to preach to the heathen and Peter to preach to the legalistic Jews.

You might be thinking, "God couldn't use me; I've been mediocre my whole life." But God doesn't plan His purposes for your life according to your previous achievements. He will always call you to do something that is beyond your natural ability, forcing you to rely on Him. If you only do what you feel you are naturally equipped to do—what you are capable of doing in your own strength and ability—then you will be tempted to give yourself the credit for success. You'll think, "I'm really good at this; I'm just a natural." In fact, I would say that if you are simply doing what comes naturally to you then you probably haven't found God's will for your life yet.

God separated Paul from his mother's womb, before he had honed his skills or accomplished anything in life. Likewise, God's purpose for you may or may not be in accordance with what you perceive as your strengths. I've heard it said that the place with the most potential on earth is a graveyard because most people die without reaching their potential; they take it to the grave.

You were separated from the womb and God put abilities in you to fulfill His purposes. But He is not going to make His will come to pass without your cooperation. You have to make an effort to find God's plan for your life. You can't judge what His plan is by merely looking at your natural abilities. If you look at your history of successes or failures, you might miss God's plan and never realize the potential He has placed inside of you.

Not Everything That's Good, Is God

Major life changes can be unsettling to contemplate, especially if you have a career and things are going well or if you are thinking about retirement and looking forward to coasting for a while. You don't want any bumps in the road. Yet here I am asking, "Have you really found the purpose God has for you?" No matter how unpleasant the thought of change may seem, it is important to know whether or not you have found your life's purpose.

I believe that most people have not found God's will for their lives. Most people are not accomplishing what God created them to do. They may be doing something good. But just because it's good, doesn't mean it's God. Not everything that is good is God's will. You may be an accomplished professional doing wonderful things, but are you doing what God has called you to do?

We each only have one chance to fulfill God's will for our lives. God's intention is not that we do whatever we want to with our lives and then, as long as our heart is pure, everything will be all right. No, you were created by God for a specific purpose that you are not going to fulfill accidentally. You have to get a revelation of what God's will is and then swim upstream to pursue it. Only with effort and time will you see God's will for your life come to pass. It isn't going to happen by fate. You have to take charge of your life and pursue God's will. You have to take control!

Find out where God wants you to go and steer your life in that direction. Jamie and I are exactly where God wants us to be, doing what He wants us to do, but we wouldn't be in the center of His will today if we had taken the easy road in the past. "*Qué será, será,*" isn't a philosophy that gets great results in life. We have sought God. We have stood against circumstances and situations that have tried to turn us away from God's will. We had to persevere. We didn't get where we are by accident or by our own strength and wisdom. It took effort. Without work and determination, I don't believe you will be able to reach the center of God's will either.

Paul said of himself, "…it pleased God, who separated me from my mother's womb, and called me by His grace" (Galatians 1:15). Paul recognized that the Lord had a purpose for him in being a representative of God. Yet for 20 or 30 years of his life, Paul thought that being a legalistic Jew was the way he would fulfill God's will. Paul said he was more zealous than anybody else and profited in the Jew's religion above many of his equals (Galatians 1:14). Finally, the Lord revealed Himself miraculously and said, "*You're doing it all wrong,*" and Paul had to completely reverse the direction his life was going.

Paul's life is proof that merely discovering some of your talents, doesn't necessarily mean that you are using them in the way God intends for you to use them. Maybe you are, but you need to hear from God to be sure. You need to find out. Life is not a dress rehearsal; it's the real deal. You will never have another today. You have to make every day count. You have to spend every day moving in the direction that God wants your life to go. You don't have time to meander through life, hoping to stumble into your purpose or praying that in the end God will use you.

It's so easy to get established in a routine. When we get a little bit of security and the pressure is off, we want to put life on cruise control. It can feel a little threatening to get out of a routine and do something new, especially if we have been doing the same thing for a long time. But we have to be willing to get out of our comfort zone in order to find God's purpose for our lives. I promise you, knowing the joy of being in the center of God's will makes it all worthwhile.

God called me to teach and minister to people. I'm doing what God has called me to do. Because of that, I can name tons of people who have been healed, marriages that have been restored, and people who have been born again. It has been awesome! But you don't have to be a minister to have a God-given purpose. The Lord has a unique purpose for everyone.

I spend millions of dollars on radio and television, yet there are people you know—friends, relatives, neighbors—who will never hear of me. It wouldn't matter if I spent ten times as much money as I am spending right now because there would still be certain people who would never hear me preach the Gospel. Some of those people might be your friends and neighbors. An ordained minister might never reach them, but you could.

You have miracles that God has appointed for you to carry out. You may never be on radio or television, and God may not use you to speak in front of thousands of people, but you have a sphere of influence that might never receive the full anointing God has for them unless you reach your potential. You don't have to mature as a Christian before God will love you. God's love is unconditional and He accepts you right where you are. But you will be happier and a much greater blessing to the people in your life, once you find your purpose and start heading in that direction.

It's possible that God wants you in the very business you're in. Not everyone who wants to live for God needs to become a full-time minister. We need believers who are out in the world, functioning in the power of God and His gifts. Becoming a pastor isn't the only way to serve God. In fact, God calls more people to be businessmen and laborers than He calls into full-time ministry. Regardless of what you are called to do, God wants you to reach people and manifest His power in the world.

You need to know that you are doing what God made you for, not simply hoping that you are doing something that is acceptable to Him. I think it would be terrible to live your whole life and not know for sure that you are doing what God created you to do. I can't imagine what that would be like. It would terrify me to go to bed and wake up, not having a clue if I am following God's will.

The only thing worse than not knowing God's will is knowing His will and choosing not to do it—either because you have talked yourself out of it or have let others talk you out of it. To know that God made you for a purpose and to feel unqualified or incapable of fulfilling it, is worse than not knowing at all.

It motivates me to know that I am doing what God created me to do. I get up in the morning with a purpose. I know I haven't achieved all that God has planned for me, but I'm progressing in the right direction. A God-given purpose and a life driven by the Holy Spirit motivate me to work through life's hardships. I don't know how people who live without a purpose find the incentive to muddle through, other than knowing that the alternative is worse. Going to work because it beats starving to death is a terrible way to live your life. You need to know that you're doing what God has called you to do. You need to live your life on purpose.

God has a purpose for every person alive. I don't care if your parents liked you or wanted you. God knew you were coming. God wrote down everything about you in His book and He has a plan for you. Every gift and talent, the time you were born, the country you were born in, and everything else about you was designed by God. You are not an accident. God has a perfect plan for your life and His plan is better than your plan for yourself.

God's Universal Will

I can tell you emphatically what God's primary will for your life is: to know Jesus. He is not willing that anyone should perish, but that all should come to repentance (2 Peter 3:9). God's will for every person on earth is to know Him. It doesn't matter what you have done in the past. Paul said he was the greatest sinner of all, yet God chose him to show that anybody who calls upon the name of the Lord will be saved (Romans 10:13). In order to be saved, or to be in right relationship with God, you must be born again.

Jesus answered and said unto him, Verily, verily, I say unto thee, Except a man be born again, he cannot see the kingdom of God.

John 3:3

You have to be certain that you are born again. A lot of church-goers in America think that merely believing God exists is enough to be saved, but the Bible says, "Thou believest that there is one God; thou doest well: the devils also believe, and tremble" (James 2:19). In other words, it's no great accomplishment to believe in God, even the devil knows that God is real. You have to do more than mentally acknowledge God's existence; you have to submit yourself to Him. You have to commit your life to Him personally and when you do that, the Bible says you are born again from above. You are changed on the inside.

If you are already born again, great, I'm not trying to talk you out of it. But if you have not committed your life to God personally, you need to. This is the first and most important step in finding God's will for your life. You need to be certain that you have done it. A lot of people think, "Well, I'm a good person. I go to church," but that isn't enough. Sitting in a church isn't going to make you a Christian, any more than sitting in a garage is going to make you a car. You must be born again.

It doesn't matter how good a person you are. All of us fall short of God's standard of perfection. You can't save yourself and that's why God became a man—Jesus—and paid the price for sin on your behalf. Nothing you can do will make you worthy of receiving God's love. No amount of good works will earn you the privilege of being righteous in God's eyes. The only thing that will restore you to a right relationship with God is putting your faith in Jesus and submitting to Him as Lord of your life.

Imagine standing before God and hearing Him ask, "What makes you worthy to enter into heaven?" How would you answer? If your first thought is to tell God what a good person you are, how you read your Bible, or that your parents used to take you to church, then you aren't born again. The only correct answer is to say, "I put my faith in Jesus Christ."

The sacrifice of Jesus Christ is what makes us right with God. In order to receive His free gift of salvation, all you have to do is believe. It's so simple that people usually think it can't be that easy. But it really is that simple. Nothing is required aside from believing in the finished work of Jesus. Scripture says,

...if thou shalt confess with thy mouth the Lord Jesus, and shalt believe in thine heart that God hath raised him from the dead, thou shalt be saved.

Romans 10:9

The words are easy to say, but you also have to believe what you say in your heart. You have to really mean that you are turning your life over to Jesus, which isn't to say that you'll never sin again. None of us are perfect and there are times when we fail. You have to be willing to turn the direction of your life over to the Lord and accept salvation solely on the basis of what Jesus has done for you.

Jesus has already paid for your sins, so salvation is simply a matter of receiving what God desires to give you. It's not a matter of trying to convince God to give you something He really doesn't want to give. Salvation is simple, but it didn't come cheap. Jesus paid for our salvation by taking the punishment we deserved in His own body on the cross. He suffered, died, and defeated death by rising again. Jesus earned salvation for us because we couldn't. So all you have to do to be saved is say this prayer out loud, believe it in your heart, and you will be born again. It's that simple.

Father, I'm sorry for my sins. I believe Jesus died to forgive my sin, and I receive that forgiveness. Jesus, I make You my Lord. I believe that You are alive, and that You now live in me. I am saved. I am forgiven. Thank You, Jesus!

God Isn't Keeping His Will a Secret

Salvation through faith in Jesus is God's universal will for every person on earth. It brings you into a personal relationship with God. It's the absolute first step in finding God's will for your life. Once you are in relationship with God, you can move on to find out what His *particular* will for your life is. God made you for one specific purpose and your only chance of reaching your full potential is to find that purpose.

Fortunately, God wants you to know and live out His will even more than you do. He desires to reveal His will to you. For the remainder of the first section of this book, we will discuss things that you can do to draw on the power of God and cause Him to reveal His will to you.

The first thing you need to do is refuse to go any further without knowing God's will for your life. As long as you can live without knowing God's purpose for your life, you will. After you insist on finding His will and commit to seeking the Lord with your whole heart, He will immediately put everything in motion to reveal Himself to you—but the first step is making a commitment.

For the which cause I also suffer these things: nevertheless I am not ashamed: for I know whom I have believed, and am persuaded that he is able to keep that which I have committed unto him against that day.

2 Timothy 1:12

God is faithful and just to keep that which we commit. No committing; no keeping. You have to commit to something. Are you going to continue to go through life thinking, "Qué será, será. Whatever will be, will be?" Or are you going to make a commitment to find God's will for your life? If you are willing to make a total commitment to seeking God and finding His perfect will for your life, then I would like to pray with you. This prayer will be a step of faith that is going to start the process of God revealing His will to you:

Father, I love you. I thank You for the knowledge that You desire to reveal Your will to me. I don't want to do things on my own anymore. Father, I want to know Your will. I want to know what You created me for. I want to take everything that I am and use it to accomplish Your purpose for me.

I know it's a process, but I am making a commitment to begin seeking and continue seeking, until I find. I'm not going to be content with living my life for myself. I now humble myself to You Lord and ask You to reveal Your will to me. Father, give me supernatural revelation.

Lord, I believe that right now the process has begun. I have made a commitment and I believe You are going to keep that which I commit. I believe You are going to draw me to a place where I will emphatically know what Your purpose and will for my life is. I thank You Father, in advance, knowing that You will reveal Yourself to me in a way that I can see and understand. I thank You for this in the name of Jesus. Amen.

Chapter 2

God of Second Chances

Our lives can get so complicated that it's hard to figure out how to get from where we are to where God wants us to be. We all make mistakes and it's easy to start thinking about what might have been if we had done just a few things differently. But I don't think it's helpful to regret things you have done and start asking yourself, "What if I would have followed God? What if I hadn't done this or that?" Satan uses thoughts like that to beat us up. Rather than reliving the past, it's better to understand that God has ways of getting us from where we are to where we need to be after we surrender our lives to Him. It's always better for us to focus on the solution instead of the problem.

The Old Testament book of First Samuel tells the story of Saul, Israel's first king. Saul's story is miraculous from the beginning. He was anointed king while he was out searching for some lost livestock. Then he stopped by to ask the prophet Samuel for help. He went there thinking that Samuel might be able to tell him where his lost donkeys were, but instead, Samuel told him that he was going to be the first king of Israel (1 Samuel 9:14-10:1). At that time however, Saul had no desire to be king.

Despite Saul's humble beginnings, he was anointed by God and became a powerful ruler. He led the nation of Israel in battle and won great victories. The people rallied around him. But two years into his reign, the Philistines gathered to fight against him in such large numbers that the men of Israel became afraid and ran off to hide in caves.

Saul regrouped the people to fight against the Philistines, then he waited for Samuel to come offer a sacrifice before leading his men into battle. (The offering was a request for the Lord's blessing before they fought the enemy). Saul waited the appointed time for Samuel to arrive, but he didn't come. The people grew restless and began to scatter. It was a crisis situation. So Saul decided to make the burnt offering himself, instead of waiting for Samuel any longer.

And Saul said, Bring hither a burnt offering to me, and peace offerings. And he offered the burnt offering. And it came to pass, that as soon as he had made an end of offering the burnt offering, behold, Samuel came; and Saul went out to meet him, that he might salute him. And Samuel said, What hast thou done? And Saul said, Because I saw that the people were scattered from me, and that thou camest not within the days appointed, and that the Philistines gathered themselves together at Michmash; Therefore said I, The Philistines will come down now upon me to Gilgal, and I have not made supplication unto the LORD: I forced myself therefore, and offered a burnt offering.

I Samuel 13:9-12

In those days, only priests who were anointed by God to offer sacrifices could make a burnt offering. We don't know what caused Samuel's delay, but regardless Saul was wrong in overstepping his bounds and moving into the office of a priest. Saul wasn't anointed to be *priest*; he was anointed to be *king*. By assuming the role of priest, he took authority that he knew he didn't have. Saul said "I forced myself," which shows that he knew it was wrong. He was admitting that normally he wouldn't have done such a thing, but the situation compelled him to do it. So he did it even though he knew it was wrong.

Saul's behavior reveals a character flaw that's true of many people today—the tendency to do whatever is in their immediate best interest, regardless of whether or not it's the right thing to do. Christians shouldn't live like that. We need to be people of integrity. If God tells us to do something, we should do it. God's will should be non-negotiable for us, regardless of the circumstances or consequences. Unfortunately, not many people live that way.

Anyone who allows an excuse to cause them to deviate from what they know is right will end up getting off course. We need to get to a place where we drive a stake in the ground and say, "This is non-negotiable. If God tells me to do something, I'll stand here and do it, even if it kills me. I will not change." We have to be uncompromising about the will of God, because we will veer off track once we start giving in to circumstances. Saul knew he wasn't supposed to offer that burnt offering, but he forced himself because it was the convenient thing to do. It might have seemed like a good reason at the time, but he knew he was disobeying God. He compromised.

And Samuel said to Saul, Thou hast done foolishly: thou hast not kept the commandment of the LORD thy God, which he commanded thee: for now would the LORD have established thy kingdom upon Israel for ever. But now thy kingdom shall not continue: the LORD hath sought him a man after his own heart, and the LORD hath commanded him to be captain over his people, because thou hast not kept that which the LORD commanded thee.

I Samuel 13:13-14

This is amazing. Samuel said that if Saul would have obeyed God that day, he would have ruled over Israel *forever*. Instead, God chose David to replace Saul as king. If Saul had obeyed God, there never would have been a King David. We never would have heard of him, because David wasn't God's first choice. Saul was not just a temporary king until David came along. Saul was God's first choice.

This incident happened in the second year of Saul's reig n (I Samuel 13:1). Then Saul reigned for another 38 years (Acts 13:21). We also know that David was 30 years old when he finally became king at the end of Saul's reign (2 Samuel 5:4). So that means that Samuel prophesied that "the Lord has sought a man after His own heart," eight years before David was even born! God said He had sought out a man after His own heart, long before David was even conceived.

David was born to be king—that was his purpose—but he wasn't God's first choice. David became king because Saul failed to do what God called him to do. But look what God did with second best! David became a mighty man of God. He was a man after God's own heart and he accomplished great things.

We can't second guess about what could have or should have been. If you have wasted time chasing your own dreams or made some bad decisions, don't get caught up in mulling over the past. Just start seeking God. Submit yourself to God. He can take wherever you are today and make His Plan B for your life better than you could ever have imagined Plan A would be. The fastest route to God's perfect will for your life is to simply start seeking Him today.

Saul's life demonstrates that God doesn't sovereignly move us around and make everything automatically work out according to His will. Saul didn't cooperate with God, therefore he missed God's will for his life. Don't get worried though—God has never had anybody qualified working for Him yet! We will all make mistakes, but God is so awesome that He can take the little bit we submit to Him and use it to accomplish His will.

Success is the Greatest Temptation

And it came to pass, after the year was expired, at the time when kings go forth to battle, that David sent Joab, and his servants with him, and all Israel; and they destroyed the children of Ammon, and besieged Rabbah. But David tarried still at Jerusalem.

2 Samuel 11:1

David was a man after God's own heart even though he didn't do everything perfectly. In those days, kings were forced to wage war when the seasons and weather allowed. This scripture says that it was time for kings to go forth to battle. David was king so he should have been leading his troops in battle. But David had become so prosperous that he didn't need to go; he had generals under him who could lead the troops for him. So David stayed home and got away from what God called him to do.

When David was running for his life from Saul and it looked like he could die at any moment, he sought God with his whole heart. After he became king, he subdued his enemies, extended the borders of the nation of Israel, and prospered greatly. God blessed him and he was more successful than any other king before him. But he stopped seeking after God wholeheartedly.

The awesome truth we need to understand here is that the greatest temptation we face in life is success. Hardship is not the worst situation in our lives. Even someone with a minimal commitment to the Lord will seek Him when the pressure is on. Failure and disaster typically drive us into the arms of God. Success is different; it makes us feel like we can make it all on our own. When everything is going good and the pressure is off, or when we don't have to seek God because it looks like everything is going our way, the contents of our heart will be revealed. Success, not failure, is the true test of character. The question is, "are you going to seek God as strongly during the good times as you do when you are struggling?

The majority of people seek the Lord more when they are in trouble. When everything is fine, they forget all about God—they don't seek Him, they don't pray, and they don't study the Word. This is what makes them more vulnerable after a victory than they are during life's struggles. When things are good they tend to forget their need for God, which leads to trouble.

And it came to pass in an eveningtide, that David arose from off his bed, and walked upon the roof of the king's house: and from the roof he saw a woman washing herself; and the woman was very beautiful to look upon. And David sent and enquired after the woman. And one said, Is not this Bathsheba, the daughter of Eliam, the wife of Uriah the Hittite? And David sent messengers, and took her; and she came in unto him, and he lay with her; for she was purified from her uncleanness: and she returned unto her house. And the woman conceived, and sent and told David, and said, I am with child.

2 Samuel 11:2-5

David was bored. He was sleeping all day, staying up all night, and not doing the things God called him to do as king. If he had been out fighting his battles, this temptation would never have come. David was bored hanging around the palace and ended up getting into trouble. He committed adultery with Bathsheba and she conceived a child. To cover up their adultery, David plotted the murder of Bathsheba's husband Uriah, who was one of the mighty men off fighting the wars David himself should have been fighting. After Uriah was dead, David took Bathsheba as his wife (2 Samuel 11:6-27).

David got himself into a pretty bad situation, which shows how even a person who has a heart for God can get way off track. The lesson for us is that when things are going well, we should seek God even more than we have been. The moment we achieve our dreams is the time we are most vulnerable to an attack. After a victory, we need to be more dependent on God than we have ever been in our lives.

The Bible says, "But the thing that David had done displeased the LORD" (2 Samuel 11:27). Boy, that's putting it mildly. God was ticked off! The Lord sent the prophet Nathan to expose what David had done. Nathan went to David and told him a story about a rich man who stole his poor neighbor's only lamb, killed it, and used it to feed a guest. David said, "Any man who would do such a thing deserves to die!" After David made his pronouncement, Nathan said "You are that man," and gave a prophecy that the child conceived by Bathsheba in adultery would die (2 Samuel 12:1-14).

I'm reading between the lines here, but I believe the reason Nathan presented the prophecy in parable form is that God was letting David prescribe his own judgment. Scripture says that God will show mercy to those who have shown mercy to others, but to those who haven't shown mercy, God will have no mercy (see James 2:13 and 2 Samuel 22:26). David knew this principle because he had written about it himself. If David had been merciful, I believe he would have received mercy in return. But because he showed no mercy to the man in this parable, David passed sentence on himself and received no mercy. As a result, the child died and there was turmoil in his household.

After the death of his baby, it says that David comforted Bathsheba and they conceived another son whom they called Solomon. The Lord loved the child and sent the prophet Nathan to announce that his name was Jedidiah (2 Sam. 12:25), which in Hebrew means "beloved of the Lord". God anointed Solomon to be David's replacement as king of Israel (1 Kings 1:17; 1 Chronicles 28:5), and he became so prosperous that he didn't even take any account of the silver in his kingdom (1 Kings 10:21).

God never wanted David and Bathsheba to have a relationship. But after it was done and they repented, God took the child born to them and blessed him. The Bible says that Solomon was the richest man who will ever live—not just the richest man of his day (2 Chronicles 1:12). It says there will never be another man who approaches the wisdom and the riches of Solomon. God knows how to work things out for good!

All of this came to a person who was totally outside of God's original plan and purpose. Saul was God's original choice; David was second best. Then David blew it! His relationship with Bathsheba was never God's will. Yet, after they repented, God blessed their marriage. Bathsheba is the virtuous woman whom Solomon wrote about in the book of Proverbs, and Solomon was greatly blessed by God.

Maybe you think you have blown it because of bad decisions you have made in the past, but you can't blow it any more than David did. Yet, God took the mess David made of his life and worked it together for good—to the extent that we remember David as a great man. He certainly had faults and problems, but overall, David was used by God in a mighty way. We still sing about "the sure mercies of David," and recognize him as the "sweet psalmist of Israel."

God did all of this with a person who wasn't His original choice. Even when this man messed up, God worked things out for good. Four or five hundred years after David died, God was still blessing the nation of Israel. He wouldn't take His mercies away from them for the sake of His servant David. God made an everlasting covenant with David, resulting in blessings to his descendants even when they weren't serving God. And all of this came through someone who missed it big-time.

I hope this encourages you. You may have made some less than perfect choices, but it is pointless to spend your time regretting the past. People have come to me and said, "I'm not sure I married the right person." It doesn't do you any good to go there now; you're married, and just like David and Bathsheba, you are committed. It would be wrong to walk away or try to reverse your life and go back. You are where you are because of the choices you have made. The thing to do is humble yourself, seek God, and realize that God can take where you are right now and work everything together for good.

God Positioning System

Regardless of what you have been through, God can take your life and make it all work out. We know that God doesn't cause the negative things in our lives, but He can still make everything turn out for good. If you have made some wrong decisions, just repent and move on. The Lord can make your life right again.

David made some serious mistakes that cost him a great deal of agony—decisions that also cost his family a lot of pain. David's daughter, Tamar, was raped by her brother, Amnon (2 Samuel 13:10-14), then David's son, Absalom, killed Amnon to avenge Tamar (2 Samuel 13:28). Eventually, Absalom tried to kill David and usurp the throne (2 Samuel 15:10). David had a lot of pain and turmoil in his life as a result of the poor decisions he made. He could have beaten himself up over his mistakes, but instead he trusted God. He chose to be strong in the grace that is in the Lord (2 Timothy 2:1). This is a great lesson for all of us.

I am absolutely convinced that regardless of where you are today or how badly you may have missed God's will for your life,

God still has a plan for you. The Apostle Paul wrote in his letter to the Romans:

> *For the gifts and calling of God are without repentance.*
>
> *Romans 11:29*

God doesn't change. Whatever His purpose for your life was when He created you, that hasn't changed either. You might be a long way from where God wants you to be right now, but God can get you where you need to be.

Modern technology allows you to have a global positioning system (GPS) in your car to help you find your way around town.

GPS devices even speak to you and tell you where to turn. But when you are driving somewhere and make a wrong turn, the GPS doesn't freak out and say, "You missed it. You'll never get there now." No, if you make a wrong turn, the GPS says, "Recalculating." It refigures your directions and tells you what to do next in order to get where you need to go; it will still get you to your destination. Missing a turn doesn't mean you need to give up and go home. God is at least as good as a GPS. It doesn't matter where you are—God can recalculate. God can take what you have done and figure a way to get you back on track. You can still get where God planned for you to go.

The gifts and the calling of God never change. You may have made some wrong turns in your life, but God's will for you has not changed. He still has a plan for you. Even if you have made a royal mess of your life, God can take what you have done and cause it to work together for good. It's sort of like a master chess player who is engaged in a chess match; it doesn't matter what move his opponent makes, the master player can always use that move to his advantage. Likewise, it doesn't matter what the devil does; it doesn't matter how much you blow it or mess up; God is able to take whatever you have done to ruin your life and turn it around.

Take Heart

I hope these biblical examples have encouraged you to take heart. God's grace is infinitely bigger than whatever you have done wrong. Your failings are no match for His grace; they aren't even worthy to mention in the same breath. You just need to humble yourself and submit your life to the Lord. Yield to Him and say, "God, here I am. Do with me what You want to." God can redeem your situation. He can redeem the lost days.

God hasn't given up on you. The simple fact that you are reading this book shows that God is drawing you and trying to reach out to you. Not a single person alive is beyond hope. No one has messed up their life so badly that God can't take it and do something supernatural with it. But you can't do things the way you always have in the past and expect different results. You're going to have to humble yourself and submit yourself to God.

Chapter 3

A Living Sacrifice

I beseech you therefore, brethren, by the mercies of God, that ye present your bodies a living sacrifice, holy, acceptable unto God, which is your reasonable service.

Romans 12:1

God used this passage of scripture to change my life. These are the very first verses that God ever spoke into my heart and made come alive. For almost 18 months leading up to that revelation, I had been seeking God and studying the Bible to find His will. I was preparing the ground. This brings up an important point I can't over emphasize: God won't reveal His will for your life until you are ready to receive it.

God doesn't show us the full scope of His plan all at once. He doesn't show us the end from the beginning. He will start pointing us in a direction and moving us toward it, but He won't show us everything all at once because we aren't ready to embrace what He has to say. Seeing the full scope of God's will all at once would overwhelm us. We might think we are incapable of doing what He has planned for us, or we might become so impatient that we would never stay the course long enough for God to prepare us to carry out our calling. It isn't that God is hesitant to show us His will; sometimes it just takes Him a while to bring us to a place where we are ready to receive it.

My preparation was seeking the Lord and being *consumed* with finding His will for my life. This hunger to know God's will led me to the verses in Romans chapter twelve. The revelation of what those verses meant led to an encounter with God on March 23, 1968. That encounter totally changed my life, and it all started with simply wanting to find God's will.

The first stage of finding God's particular will for your life is to become a living sacrifice, holy and acceptable unto Him (Romans 12:1). From an eternal perspective, what you do for an occupation is incidental. The Lord doesn't want your *service* as much as He wants *you*. He loves you more than He loves what you can do for Him. Now, that's an important point to make, because in our day and age—especially in the type of church atmosphere that I grew up in—it's all about service, a push to *do* something for God. It's true that you were created for God's pleasure and glory, but God's acceptance of you is not related to what you do for Him. The Lord sacrificed Himself so He could have *you*, not your *service*.

When I was seeking God in 1968, I wasn't even thinking about being a preacher. I was asking God if He wanted me to be a teacher, doctor, or something like that. One of the things the Lord spoke to me was that I was missing it by seeking Him for a vocation. He told me, "I want you; if I get you, then I'll be able to use you however I want to." I was praying "Oh, God, use me. Show me what You want me to do. God, should I do this or that?" The Lord finally spoke to me and said, "The reason I haven't used you is because you aren't usable. Quit praying that I'll use you; pray 'God, make me usable.'"

Besides, God wants to use you more than you want to be used. If you make yourself a living sacrifice and commit your life to the Lord, I guarantee you He will start developing your talents and directing you. As soon as you get usable, God will use you. Jesus said to His disciples,

The harvest truly is plenteous, but the labourers are few; Pray ye therefore the Lord of the harvest, that he will send forth labourers into his harvest.

Matthew 9:37-38

God is looking for people He can use, but the problem is most of us aren't usable. Of course, making ourselves usable doesn't mean that we try to go out and accomplish God's plan in our own strength and ability. Look how Jesus approached His ministry:

Now when he was in Jerusalem at the Passover, in the feast day, many believed in his name, when they saw the miracles which he did. But Jesus did not commit himself unto them, because he knew all men, and needed not that any should testify of man: for he knew what was in man.

John 2:23-25

What would we do if this happened today? Let's say, for instance, a preacher came to your town and suddenly people were being raised from the dead and miracles were happening by the hundreds. What would the average preacher do in that situation? He would probably mobilize the people, put literature in their hands, and send them out to witness to others about the power of God they were seeing. Then he would call the television stations, advertise, and try to take advantage of what was happening.

This scripture describes a multitude of people who were willing to acknowledge that Jesus was the Christ. Yet, Jesus did not commit Himself to them. He didn't partner with them because He knew what was in man. Jesus didn't want those people talking about Him because He knew they weren't ready. For one thing, they weren't born again. They weren't filled with the Holy Spirit either. Even after His disciples had spent three and a half years with Him and had seen Him rise from the dead, the last thing Jesus told them was, "Don't go tell anybody I'm resurrected from the dead until you receive the power of the Holy Spirit. Then you'll be empowered to be My witnesses." (see Acts 1:4-5,8)

Jesus is more concerned about the *quality* of ministry than He is the *quantity* of ministry. We're almost completely the opposite. Today when someone gets born again, we pat them on the back and immediately send them out to tell everybody. That isn't the way God wants the church to operate.

You need to be prepared. You need to get to where you aren't ministering out of your own ability, but through the power of God.

It takes a while for that to happen. Jesus wouldn't commit Himself to those people because He didn't want anyone to speak out of their own ability. The majority of people today who represent God are just teaching things they have heard someone else say. Their hearts may be good and they may mean well, but their teaching is just the teaching of men. It's not the power of the Holy Spirit, therefore it causes problems.

This goes right along with the idea that God wants you before He wants your service. If God doesn't have your heart then why would He want to reveal His purpose to you? You would just go out in your own human ability and make a mess of things, trying to fulfill His will. He loves you too much for that. Sure the Lord is concerned about the witness you present to others, but it is also out of love and concern for you that He doesn't want you stepping out solely in your own power.

Fight in God's Strength

Some wonderful things go along with finding God's will. Earlier, I mentioned a sense of satisfaction, peace, and joy that you will never experience unless you find God's will. When you find God's plan and walk in the center of His will, it's like pinning a huge target on yourself. Satan fights against those who try to advance the kingdom of God. You are going to be met with opposition while fulfilling God's purpose for your life. You will face challenges. If God doesn't have your heart so He can mold it to meet your needs and give you faith to overcome obstacles, you're going to be in trouble. The wiles of the enemy and the darts that come against you would destroy you if you found God's will and moved out in your own strength to accomplish it.

The reason that some people haven't bumped into the devil is because they're going in the same direction! They haven't had any great problems in life because they aren't a threat. The good news is that, as far as we can tell in Scripture, demons don't reproduce. So either there was a bunch of demons per person back in Adam and Eve's day or there's a shortage of demons today. Personally, I believe there's a shortage of demons. I believe Satan is short-handed and I don't believe, as some claim, that every person has their own personal demon.

Satan taught a lot of us a couple wrong things a long time ago so now we're doing a wonderful job messing up our own lives. He can leave us alone because we're doing a bang up job destroying our lives on our own. Some people have probably inspired the devil. I bet the devil sometimes sits down and takes notes and says, "Oh, I never thought of that one." Seriously though, when you find God's will and the anointing of God flows through you and people's lives are impacted, I can guarantee that you are going to face some form of demonic activity.

Satan puts a priority on people who are in the center of God's will, making an impact, and causing his earthly kingdom damage. It's just like being in a battle: an army that is attacked on one flank will shift forces to reinforce that area and repel the attack. In the same way, when you start fulfilling God's will for your life there is going to be opposition. Satan will marshal his forces against you to protect himself. God loves you too much to reveal His will to you and put you on the front lines when you are not prepared to meet the challenge.

I hope you are getting this. One of the main reasons God doesn't automatically reveal His will to everyone is that He loves us too much to put us at risk. He doesn't want us out there trying to advance His kingdom in our flesh, unable to deal with the opposition and criticism that comes against us. He doesn't want us to be destroyed. He's not willing to sacrifice us. God doesn't see us as a disposable commodity. He doesn't use people like you would a straw in a soda cup: suck on it until you hear *sluuurrrp*, then throw the cup away, and go get another one. God loves us too much to use us like that. He loves us more than He loves what we can do for Him.

Self-Centeredness Is the Root of All Evil

To become a living sacrifice, you have to die to yourself and your own selfish ambitions. A sacrifice is something you place on the altar. It doesn't give instructions; it is at the mercy of the person doing the sacrificing. The sacrificer can do anything he wants with the sacrifice. Dying to one's *self* isn't normal. It isn't what fallen human beings naturally desire.

In case you haven't noticed, sweet little babies don't give a rip about anything but their own needs. They scream and cry to wake mom up in the middle of the night to be fed, oblivious to the fact that mommy just went through labor and is exhausted. Babies will do whatever it takes to get what they want, when they want it, and they don't care one bit how it affects others. Babies think they are the center of the universe. Every one of us came into the world exactly that way, and sad to say, a majority of us are still that way.

We might not fall on the floor and suck our thumb or throw a fit, but we still act in selfish ways. Adults have different ways of being self-centered, like turning a shoulder to our spouse that is cold enough to form icicles. The natural tendency of fallen human beings is to think that the world revolves around them. This selfish tendency is Satan's beachhead into your life. It's how he gains access to you.

Satan's temptation against Adam and Eve was to get them to think about themselves. Basically, his temptation was saying to them, "God isn't thinking about you, He's keeping something from you. You could be more like God." In truth however, God created a perfect world for Adam and Eve and there wasn't a single reason for them to be upset. The Garden of Eden was perfect. God Almighty walked with Adam and Eve in the cool of the evening. He gave them honor and respect. Everything was absolutely perfect, but Satan made them think that God was holding something back. Adam and Eve rejected God because they didn't think what they had was good enough—they wanted more.

All human beings start out selfish but we don't have to stay that way. Prior to my encounter with the Lord in 1968, I was doing all the *right* things for all the *wrong* reasons. I was an absolute hypocrite and didn't even realize it. As far as I knew, I was the most religious kid in our church. I led two or three people a week to the Lord, I started a special youth visitation, I went to the adult visitation, I witnessed to people, I did everything I could. I lived at church and I was seeking God with everything I knew, but the Lord showed me that I was doing it all for myself and a little pat on the back.

On March 23, 1968, God pulled back a curtain and showed me that my heart was all wrong. He showed me that I was selfish and had not been seeking Him with pure motives. We had a prayer meeting every Saturday night. Here I was, an 18-year-old boy meeting every Saturday night to pray with my friends—that should give you an indication of how religious I was! We were in this prayer meeting joking around, when the youth director of our church came in and dropped to his knees on the floor of the pastor's study. He started praying and crying out to God for about 45 minutes. During his prayer, I was kneeling down across the room, but instead of enjoying his prayer or communing with God, I was caught up in myself. *How rude,* I thought. *He just came in here and now he's praying on and on. What am I going to pray?"* I asked myself, *There won't be anything left to say by the time he finishes! Everybody is going to think I'm carnal and don't love God.*

I was thinking these things, when I suddenly realized what an absolute hypocrite I was. I saw how self-centered my whole life had been. I don't know how it happened, it was supernatural, but it was like God just pulled a curtain back. I saw how everything I thought I had been doing for the Lord was actually for my own benefit. I started confessing all of the self-centered things I was seeing about myself; I turned myself inside out in front of my best friends and all the leaders of the church. I thought nobody was ever going to want to be around me again after hearing the things I was revealing—all of the lust and hate that was in my heart—and the way I thought of other people. I ruined my reputation, but I didn't care. I knew I needed to get right with God.

Before this experience, I had been proud of my performance. Now I saw my self-righteousness from God's perspective and thought He was about to kill me. I was just trying to confess everything I could think of, so when He killed me I could go to heaven. I thought God was seeing all of that junk for the first time—just like I was. I prayed and confessed for about an hour and a half. It was probably the first time in my life I had prayed more than 15 minutes at a time.

When I was through, there was nothing left to say, nothing more I could give, nothing left to confess. I made myself a living sacrifice that night. I humbled myself. I saw that God was righteous, and I was unrighteous. I expected God to kill me because of how unrighteous I was. But instead of wrath and rejection, the tangible love of God came over me and changed my life. It was so real! For a period after that night, I never slept more than an hour at a time and I never sat down to eat a meal; I just ate enough to keep me going. I was excited; I couldn't sleep knowing how much God loved me! How could I sit down and eat when I could be reading the Bible?

Experiencing God's love transformed my life. Instead of the rejection and punishment I thought was coming, God showed me that He loved me and I knew it had nothing to do with me. For the first time in my life, I saw that I was a "zero with the rim knocked off." I found God's love and realized it was solely according to His grace. It had nothing to do with my goodness or badness. God just loved me. Learning this truth totally changed me.

Not everybody is going to have the same kind of dramatic encounter that I did, but everybody needs to have a similar experience; a time when you make the decision to quit sitting on the throne of your life, trying to determine your own future. We become a sacrifice when we hand over control, which is primarily what God wants to accomplish in all of us. Until we reach that place, God can't reveal His perfect will—or He certainly can't reveal the entirety of it—because we would go out and try to accomplish it in our own strength and would end up getting hurt or hurting others.

God wants your heart more than He wants your service. You need to run up a white flag of surrender and say, "God, I'm yours. I'll do anything you want." I guarantee you that God's plan for you is better than your plan for yourself. It will take a period of time for you to be able to learn God's plan and for Him to work some things out in you. The Lord will start you on the most adventurous path you could ever dream. Life will be better than you could ever plan for yourself.

Yielding to the Lord isn't a one-time decision. The initial resolution begins the process, but God can't deal with all of your flesh in one moment. You have to keep making the choice to surrender. The only way for you to never have another problem with your flesh is for you to physically die. As long as you are breathing, you have a self, and that carnal nature is going to seek to reassert its desires.

I haven't been perfect since March 23, 1968, when I surrendered my life to God. I haven't always loved God flawlessly and avoided all selfishness. But I made a commitment with all of my heart that night. As soon as I see selfishness rise up in my life, I repent. I've had to say, "Whoops, there's *self* coming back up again. Father, I'm not going that way. Thank You for showing me." I've had to get back on track, but I've never lost my commitment. I committed myself to God in 1968 and have not been uncommitted since. I haven't always lived up to my commitment, but I've never had to start over again.

Today, most people just commit a little bit, then they do something in absolute rebellion against God and have to come back and recommit. Their lives are up and down like a yo-yo. But we can reach a place where we literally turn everything over to God and that's all there is to it—a place where no matter what God tells us to do, we will do it without discussion.

When the Lord first called Jamie and me to go to Pritchett, Colorado, I didn't have any desire to go there. It was a puny town of 144 people, 30 miles away from the next largest town of

1,000. As a matter of fact, the first time we drove through Pritchett we were with some friends of ours and I started laughing and saying, "Don, I think God's calling you here." I said, "Thus saith the Lord…" and I started joking with him about being called to Pritchett. But it wasn't two months later that *I* was living there!

I had some resistance to the idea, but the moment I was sure God wanted me to do it, I did it. I didn't understand everything. Going to pastor a church of ten people in a town of 144 people wasn't a stepping stone to anything. The only way you leave a situation like that is feet first. But I knew God wanted me to do it, so I did. Once I committed to following God's leading to go to Pritchett, God put His desires in my heart and I fell in love with the place. I loved Pritchett and had a great time there.

A few times in my life, I have struggled to know if what I was feeling led to do was really God. But once I knew it was God's will, it was non-negotiable for me—I just did it. I have discovered that most people aren't like that which is one of the reasons God hasn't revealed His will to them yet. It's also the reason they are struggling. It solves a lot of problems when you figure out that there's only one God, and you aren't Him! As long as you are playing God in your life, picking and choosing what you do, you aren't a living sacrifice.

The heart of God's will for you is to be a living sacrifice, committed unto Him. Once you reach that place, you will have to rebel against God to keep from seeing His good, acceptable, and perfect will come to pass in your life (Romans 12:2). God doesn't need a silver vessel. He's looking for a surrendered vessel. Commit your life to Him and He will promote you in whatever area He wants you to go. You will prosper and have the favor of God. Things will work better than they ever did when you were the one calling the shots. Believe it or not, God is smarter than you! God knows more than you do. He can direct your life better than you can (Jeremiah 10:23), so don't lean unto your own understanding (Proverbs 3:5).

Fully submitting to God is the starting place. You can't get around this step. Most people want to skip this rung and move on up to the top of the ladder; they want to stride right into the center of God's will and see great things happen. You're not going to get far that way. The reason we have people in ministry who wind up committing adultery and stealing money is because they didn't take the time to build a foundation of character and integrity. They didn't wait on God to promote them, so fame corrupted them. Don't make that mistake by trying to get around becoming a living sacrifice. Selfishness is Satan's inroad to your life; it's how he gains access to you.

Most people don't trust God to advance them in life because they're too busy trying to advance themselves. In general, we demand respect and assert our rights in an attempt to make everyone around us realize how important we are. This is pretty much the opposite of being a living sacrifice. Being committed to God doesn't mean we lie down like a doormat every time we are confronted with a problem. If God tells us to do something to change our circumstances, we need to do it. I'm just saying that we shouldn't be motivated by selfish desires.

A Living Sacrifice

Being a living sacrifice is the first step in finding God's will. It would really jump start your spiritual life to get off the throne and say, "Jesus, I want *You* to control my life." Still, it's a process. If you are living a totally selfish life right now, you have a lot of momentum built up in that direction. You can't make a complete U-turn instantly. If the Lord suddenly turned you around, it would be a disaster—like trying to flip a U-turn while going 65 mph on the highway. It's going to take God some time to turn you around and get you moving in the right direction.

The starting point is for you to be willing to allow God to begin the change. Even after you make a commitment with all of your heart, you're still going to have a "self" to deal with. You don't get delivered of your "self." The only way you can get delivered from your carnal self is to die physically.

Making Course Corrections

Jim Erwin was one of the astronauts who walked on the moon. I was in Vietnam when all of that was going on, but I always wanted to know more about it. One day, I was on a television program with Jim and had the opportunity to talk to him about the lunar landing. I thought the technology was so awesome, blasting off for the moon and landing on the exact spot they were aiming for.

But as I talked to Jim, I learned it wasn't like that at all. He said that NASA basically threw the capsule towards the moon and every ten minutes for four days, they had to adjust their direction in order to stay on course. Sometimes the capsule was 90 degrees off from the direction it needed to be traveling, so they had to fire up the rocket to get back on track. Other times they were just a fraction of an inch off.

The flight path to the moon wasn't a straight line; it was a jumble of zigzags. Jim said they had a 500-mile-long target area for their landing. When he got out of the lunar module and stepped onto the moon, he was within five feet of being outside the landing zone. They nearly missed a 500 mile landing strip! But they still made it.

As Jim was telling me this, the Lord spoke to me and said, "That's the way it is when you make a commitment of your life to Me." It's not like you commit once and never make another mistake. You make a total commitment, and within five or ten minutes, you are going to have an opportunity for a course correction. Somebody is going to cut in front of you in line at the grocery store, cut you off in traffic, or say something rude. You will have the opportunity to make a course correction every ten minutes for the rest of your life!

The problem with a living sacrifice is that it keeps trying to crawl off the altar. You need to make a total commitment. Don't be surprised if you wake up one morning thinking, "What about me? What about my desires and ambitions?" It doesn't mean you weren't committed to God or that you won't make it. It just means that you still have "flesh" that needs to be subdued. Just deny your flesh and make a course correction.

You will experience the beginning of God when you come to the end of yourself, which isn't to say that you can't encounter God every once in a while or that He can't touch you. God loves you and He will move in your life as much as you let Him. But you aren't going to see the miraculous power of God consistently working in your life until you quit trying to do everything yourself and put Him first.

We are totally self-centered when we come out of the womb. If you have never taken the step of putting God first, you are *still* self-centered. You might be a 20, 30, 40, or 60 year-old adult brat who still thinks that life is all about *you*. You've heard the joke about how many people it takes to change a light bulb, right? In most cases, the answer is "just one," because the person holds the bulb and the world revolves around them—or at least that's what they think.

God created us to live for a greater purpose than just satisfying our own needs. We need to humble ourselves and make ourselves a living sacrifice. That's not all there is to fulfilling God's will, but you can't do anything else until you take this first step. Some people make a total commitment to God and then get off course. If you made a total commitment to God in the past, then maybe He is just trying to tell you, "Hey, you're off track." No big deal; just make a course correction and get back to the commitment you already made to follow God.

The vast majority of people who are searching for God's will have probably never turned control of their lives over to the Lord.

If you're thinking, "I'm an adult brat. I'm totally self-centered. My whole life has been about me," then you need to make a commitment to God. Allow God to give you guidance about the direction to take with your future. If there is any doubt in your mind about whether or not you have made a total commitment to God then you haven't done it. If you are feeling a tug on your heart to make a commitment, I suggest you respond now while the Holy Spirit is leading you.

Becoming a living sacrifice isn't only for the "super-saints" or those who *really* want to seek God; every born-again believer is supposed to be a living sacrifice. Sadly, a lot of our churches are promoting "self-help" philosophies as the way to happiness. But the Christian life isn't about having a positive self-image; it's the Christ-image in us that matters. We need to exalt Christ, not "self."

If you are willing to say, "I need to become a living sacrifice." If you are willing to start moving in that direction and want to give God the right to start running your life, you can make that commitment right now. Thank God for showing you the next step. Acknowledge that you are not capable of dying to yourself in your own strength. Determine to become a living sacrifice and trust the Lord to start leading you out of selfishness and into His plans for your life. Give God the freedom to show you the way you should go and then resolve to follow His leading.

I believe that as you humble yourself under the mighty hand of God, He will lift you up. As you turn your life over to Him, He will begin a process of renewal. This step you are taking is not merely a mental acknowledgement of God's supremacy; it's a supernatural restoration process through which Jesus will begin to dominate your focus. The moment you make this decision, you will begin to recognize how God is moving in your life to bless you and give you direction. I believe that as you turn your life over to God, He will touch your heart and you will never be the same.

Chapter 4

Renewing Your Mind

Becoming a living sacrifice is important, but having a renewed mind is equally important. Without a renewed mind, you will end up missing God's perfect will for your life. A commitment to go anywhere and do anything for God can leave you vulnerable to the devil's manipulation, unless you balance your commitment with knowledge of the truth in God's Word.

At the time God told me to quit school and I ended up being sent to Vietnam, I had some wrong ideas about the true nature of God. When I was growing up, it had been instilled in me by the church I attended that nothing could happen unless God allowed it to, so I thought that whatever happens in life must be God's will. I didn't understand that we have an enemy and that God isn't the source of the evil in our world. While I was in Vietnam, I spent a lot of time studying the Word, but I still didn't learn the truth that God doesn't tempt people with evil, that He's only the source of good (James 1:13, 17).

Right after I came home from Vietnam, a traveling minister who had seven incurable diseases came to preach at our church.

While he was there, he went to a doctor friend of mine who ran an EKG on him and sent it to the lab for analysis. The lab came back and said, "Is this a joke? You sent us an EKG on a dead guy!"

This minister had seven diseases and an EKG reading that showed he was dead, yet he was alive and preaching at our church. Granted, he was just barely alive. He was struggling. He couldn't stand on his feet so he just sat in a chair and preached for an hour or two. The basic message he preached was that "Satan is God's messenger boy." He was saying that Satan couldn't do anything unless God allowed it; therefore, if you had a problem, God allowed it in your life to teach you something and help you grow.

At that time I was committed to God and ready to do anything, and here's a guy with seven incurable diseases preaching that God uses Satan to teach us things. As I was listening to him I started thinking, U*h-oh, what if God wants to teach me something?* Jamie and I were engaged, so during the week this traveling preacher was at our church, I went to the doctor to get a routine exam for our marriage license. The exam revealed that I had yellow jaundice. The doctor said, "If you don't lie flat on your back for a month you could get really sick." He told me that physical exertion could kill me or put me in a coma. But I determined I wasn't going to lie on my back for a month. I was trying to believe God for healing.

After I learned about my health problem, this traveling minister took me and twelve or fifteen other people from the church out to eat. We were all sitting together and during the meal he started to prophesy over me. He said, "You're going to go into a coma. You'll be in a coma for eight years." He went on to talk about how God was putting me into a coma to make me holy, and when I came out I would be like the apostle Paul because God would have shown me great revelations. He said that God was going to judge me and do all of this to break me.

I was in tears as I listened to him speak all of that death and destruction over me. I had made a total commitment to God, so I thought, *Well, if this is God's will, I accept it.* I believed everything that preacher was saying. The devil had me convinced that God was going to use sickness to teach me a lesson—but he went too far. If he would have quit right there, you never would have heard of me. I probably would have gone into that coma and died.

He had me on the ropes, but he just wouldn't quit. The preacher kept pouring it on. He kept talking about how terrible all of the suffering was on him, and finally he said, "The worst thing about this is that God has put me on a fast from the Bible for eight years. He told me that for eight years I can't read the Word. The only time I open the Bible is when I preach to other people." When he said that, it grabbed my attention. I didn't know a lot back then, but I knew better than to believe that God would tell someone not to read the Bible.

I was in love with God and excited about the Word. I had just come home from Vietnam where I had spent the majority of every day reading the Bible. God's Word was my meditation day and night. The minute that preacher said those things, I stood up and said, "I reject this in the name of Jesus. I am not accepting this stuff. I don't understand everything but I know God would never put me on a fast from the Word of God." Jamie and I left that church, we left our closest friends, and we walked away from that teaching. Praise God, I knew just enough truth to recognize that he was preaching a lie.

You need to be a living sacrifice. If you don't renew your mind to the truth, Satan will take advantage of your desire to do anything for God. You need to balance your commitment to the Lord with a revelation of truth that comes from His Word. Jamie and I avoided a disaster because we had renewed our minds just enough to know God would never tell us not to read His Word. But what would have happened if we didn't know that truth? I don't have to imagine. I have a perfect example.

Two years earlier, I heard this same minister teach the same things. I brought his teaching entitled, "Satan Is God's Messenger Boy" home and gave it to my girlfriend. She happened to be one of Jamie's best friends and loved God with all of her heart. She had also made a commitment to be a living sacrifice to the Lord.

In his teaching, the minister used an example of a boy who wanted to be a witness for the Lord but was shy and introverted. He found it hard to witness to his football buddies, so he prayed and asked the Lord to give him an incurable disease so he could show them he wasn't afraid of death. Sure enough, at his funeral, four of his football teammates got born again because of his testimony.

As a result of listening to this teaching, my girlfriend prayed a similar prayer and the next morning she had to be rushed to the hospital. She was diagnosed with acute leukemia and believed the Lord had given this to her as an answer to her prayer in order to break her and glorify Himself. I had gone off to Vietnam during this time and although we were only officially boyfriend and girl-friend, her parents said we were engaged and got me an emergency leave to come home and be with her during her final days.

I was with her when she hemorrhaged and strangled to death on her own blood. It was devastating, but at the time, we thought this was God's will. Sure enough, at her funeral four people gave their lives to the Lord. Of course, I now know God didn't do this, nor did He allow it. We allowed it because of our wrong beliefs. The Lord used this situation to bring some people to Himself, but he didn't cause it. Satan used this to hurt a number of people who are still reeling from it today. Our hearts may have been good but our minds were wrong. This demonstrates how being a living sacrifice can be dangerous if we don't have our mind renewed with the truth of God's Word.

You Choose the Mold

And be not conformed to this world: but be ye transformed by the renewing of your mind, that ye may prove what is that good, and acceptable, and perfect, will of God.

Romans 12:2

The Greek word that is translated *conformed* in this verse means "to pour into a mold." As Christians, we shouldn't be poured into the mold of this world. This reminds me of when I was drafted into the Army and received orders to go to Vietnam. I was sitting in a room along with everyone else who had been drafted at the same time. The officials came in and told us we were going to war and a lot of the guys started crying. So they called in a chaplain and he said, "The army is a fire and it will melt you. But you get to pick what mold you fit into."

I realized right then that I wasn't going to come out of the Army the same man I was when I went in. The experience was going to melt me, but I was going to pick the mold. I was going to choose to be conformed to the image of Jesus. I took that chaplain's message to heart and came out of the Army ten times stronger in the Lord than I was when I went in.

In the same way, the experiences of life are going to melt you. You aren't going to leave this world with the same mentality you had when you came into it. Life is going to test you. You are going to be melted. But you get to pick the mold you get squeezed into. As Christians we need to be molded into the image of Christ.

The way to keep from being conformed to the image of this world is through the renewing of your mind. The scripture says, "...be ye transformed by the renewing of your mind...." The Greek word for "transform" in that passage is metamorphoō, which is the same word we get metamorphosis from; the process of a caterpillar spinning a cocoon and emerging a little while later as a butterfly. It's a word picture for our lives. If you want to change from something that is earth bound to something that is flying and beautiful—if you want *metamorphosis*—you have to renew your mind.

The Seed of God's Word

This is so simple that you have to have somebody help you to misunderstand it, yet a lot of the church is missing this point. Most people are praying, "Oh, God, please change everything. Please help my finances. Help my marriage to work out." People know that God can do anything so they ask Him to rearrange their entire lives in an instant. But not everything happens by prayer alone. I'm not discounting prayer. I believe in the power of prayer. I'm just saying that Scripture says we are born again by the incorruptible seed of God's Word (1 Peter 1:23). Jesus taught that the sower sows the Word. He told His disciples that unless they understood that simple principle they wouldn't understand any of His parables (Mark 4:13-14).

The world we live in operates on the cycle of seeds giving birth to new growth that matures until it can also reproduce by seed. Everything in nature comes from a seed: plants, animals, and people are all born of a seed. Jesus taught that the kingdom of God also operates like a seed (Matthew 13:31). The seed you have to plant to get kingdom results is the Word of God (Luke 8:11). If you want to have prayers regularly answered, you have to sow the Word. The Word of God shows you God's way of thinking. It renews your mind and tears down the obstacles that prevent us from freely receiving all that Christ has already purchased for us.

When people come to me for healing prayer I often ask them, "What are you doing in response to this sickness?" Typically they will say they have gone to the doctor, taken medication, and prayed. But what I really want to know is, what are they basing their faith on? What seeds have they sown? What scriptures have they used to renew their minds to God's truth? It seems like not one person in a hundred mentions the Word of God. So I'll say, "What scripture are you basing your faith on?" Usually I get a response like, "Well, I think it says someplace that by Jesus' stripes we're healed. Isn't that what it says?" Such a limited understanding of God's Word won't get you far.

The scripture says that by renewing your mind, you are transformed—changed from a creepy crawly thing to something beautiful that can fly. The majority of believers aren't renewing their minds. Most people let their minds be polluted by focusing on what's happening in the world. Consequently, they get squeezed into the mold of the world.

On September 11, 2001, after the terrorist attacks happened, there were Christians who wouldn't fly because they were just as afraid as the unbelievers. Fear struck their hearts when the Bible says very clearly, let not your heart be troubled (John 14:1). The psalmist wrote, "God is our refuge and strength, a very present help in trouble. Therefore will not we fear, though the earth be removed, and though the mountains be carried into the midst of the sea" (Psalm 46:1-2). This is saying that even if all of the seas cover the earth, we will not be fearful. This is how the Word of God tells us to react. Yet whenever disaster strikes, Christians get into the same fear as unbelievers because they are poured into the mold of this world, instead of having their minds renewed by the Word of God and being poured into His image.

Meditating on the Word will make you think differently than the world. You won't be squeezed into the same mold. You will begin to see things differently and have a different attitude. Christians ought to be different than unbelievers. We shouldn't have the same fear-based reactions as people who don't know Jesus. We are spiritually alive; they are spiritually dead—that's a big difference. The difference between a live person and a dead person should be clear for all to see.

If all of the average Christians in America were arrested, there wouldn't be enough evidence of their beliefs to convict them in a court of law. Believers are just as sick and poor as their neighbors who don't know God. When the layoffs come, Christians are just as afraid of what's going to happen as unbelievers. I'm not saying this to make anyone feel condemned or unworthy. I'm just trying to point out that we have been squeezed into the mold of this world. But we should be a lot different than unbelievers. The reason we aren't different is because we haven't transformed ourselves by the renewing of our minds. We watch *As the Stomach Turns* on television and adopt the world's way of thinking as truth, instead of adopting God's way of thinking.

The Truth Will Set You Free

And ye shall know the truth, and the truth shall make you free.

John 8:32

Jesus said that the Word of God is the truth (John 17:17). The truth is what sets you free, and it's only the truth you *know* that sets you free. You can't just keep the Bible under your arm or on your bedside table and say, "Oh, I believe the Bible." You have to read it and know what it says.

At Charis Bible College, we have a reading program in which our students read the Bible through in one year. Every year some students complain about that, so I tell them, "This is a *Bible* College. I think you should at least read the Bible by the time you graduate." The majority of people who come to the Bible school have probably never read the entire Bible, yet most of them say they believe it.

A lot of people are worried that the Word will lose its freshness or it will become boring like a novel if they read it all, but that will never happen. I've read through the Bible hundreds of times and I get more out of it every time I read it. It almost seems like you have to spend 30 years in the Bible just to learn enough to ask the right questions. I'm just now beginning to understand the Word in ways I never have before. So even if you have read the Bible once, I guarantee that you didn't get it all. You need to be studying the Word and renewing your mind with it on a daily basis.

Many people come to me and say, "I'm powerless. I can't do anything. Would you please pray for me?" But I don't have any special power that they don't have. God has given every born-again believer the same authority. Once you recognize who you are in Christ, you can take your authority, speak to your body, and command sickness to leave. The Bible says, "Resist the devil, and he will flee from you" (James 4:7). The average Christian doesn't realize what God has already done for him, so he goes to God like a beggar—pleading for an answer to prayer. We need to get rid of that stinking thinking because it's killing us.

If Jesus were here in His physical body today, He would not be pleased with our inability. In the 17th chapter of the Gospel of Matthew, Jesus' disciples brought a man to Him because they had been unable to cast a demon out of the man's son. Jesus didn't say to them, "Oh, don't feel bad about yourself. It's My fault, I shouldn't have left you alone." No, Jesus called them a faithless and perverse group of people and said, "How long shall I be with you? How long shall I suffer you? Bring him hither to me" (Matthew 17:17).

This incident occurred before Jesus died and rose again—before anyone could be born again and become a temple of the Holy Spirit. At the time of that story, the disciples didn't have the advantages we have: we have born-again spirits, we are empowered by the Holy Spirit to do the works that Jesus did, and we have the truth of God's Word at our fingertips. Yet, the sick people who come to us for healing aren't always being delivered to the degree that they should be. Jesus told us to meet the needs of people, but we aren't even coming close.

As You Think, So You Are

For as he thinketh in his heart, so is he…

Proverbs 23:7

Transformation comes by renewing the mind, so in order to experience positive changes in our lives, we need to change the way we think. That's what I mean by getting rid of *stinking thinking*. Our lives go in the direction of our dominant thoughts so we need to make sure our thoughts line up with what we desire. Believing that we have Christ's "raising-from-the-dead" power living inside of us makes it a lot more likely that we will see miraculous results when we pray. If we don't believe that we have authority over sickness, we are not likely to see very good results when we tell sickness to leave our bodies. As we think, that's the way we are (Proverbs 23:7). If we think we are powerless, we will be.

It saddens me to see how far below their privileges the average Christian lives. They believe they will be healed if I or another minister prays for them. But they haven't renewed their mind to believe God will do it for them. I've seen all kinds of healings and miracles, but I don't have a special anointing for healing. I don't have anything that "Joe-Blow-believer" doesn't have. The only reason I might see better results than most people is because I know what God has given me and I use it.

God Almighty lives on the inside of every believer, yet we act like He's out in space somewhere. We think the devil is blocking our prayers from getting through to God, so we do "spiritual warfare" and get a hundred million people to pray and open up the heavens so our prayers can get through. We don't need to do that. God isn't waiting for us to try hard enough before He answers our prayers. No, God lives on the inside of us and He says that He is never going to leave us nor forsake us (Hebrews 13:5). We don't have to get our prayers past demons in order for them to reach God or enlist enough prayer warriors to force God to listen to our prayers. Weird doctrines like that only come up because we don't know what the Word says.

Have you ever heard the expressions, *What you don't know won't hurt you,* or *Ignorance is bliss?* Well, both of those statements are lies. What you don't know *is* killing you. We've been squeezed into the mold of the world and our ignorance of the truths in God's Word *is* killing us. You have to renew your mind if you want to find, follow, and fulfill your God-given purpose in life. Making a commitment to the Lord is a start, but you have to get into the Word of God. You need to get to where you know God's Word better than you know what's happening on your favorite TV show. I enjoy watching the old cartoon *Wile E. Coyote and the Road Runner.* I think it's funny. But if that's all I'm full of then in a crisis situation when I open my mouth, all that will come out is "Beep, Beep!!" And I'm going to be in trouble.

Whatever we focus our attention on is what will dominate our thoughts (Proverbs 23:7). If our thoughts are dominated by the things of this world then we are going to get worldly results in our lives. We need to focus on God to get godly results. That's why Jesus admonished us to "seek first the kingdom of God." (Matthew 6:33). We shouldn't be absorbed by what's going on in the world, by all of this stuff that doesn't amount to anything. We need to have an eternal focus.

People who are struggling and haven't seen God's will manifest in their lives probably haven't renewed their minds to God's way of thinking. Don't be discouraged if you suspect that you fall into that category. Now that you know what the problem is, you can fix it. Renew your mind with the Word of God and you will prove the good, acceptable, and perfect will of God. It's that simple. Having done that, you would have to rebel against God to miss His will for your life. After you renew your mind, you can count on seeing God's will come to pass in your life. All you have to do is commit yourself to the Word of God and you will see some awesome things begin to happen.

Chapter 5

Your Spiritual Identity

I can't over-emphasize how essential the Word of God is in discovering our spiritual identity and finding God's will for our lives. A lot of people look at the Bible and think, "This book was written thousands of years ago, what does it have to do with me?" The Bible isn't just another book, it is quick—which means alive—and powerful. It reveals things to us that we could never figure out on our own.

> *For the word of God is quick, and powerful, and sharper than any two-edged sword, piercing even to the dividing asunder of soul and spirit, and of the joints and marrow, and is a discerner of the thoughts and intents of the heart.*
>
> *Hebrews 4:12*

This scripture implies that to know the difference between soul and spirit is hard. And it is. In fact, most people don't know the difference. Functionally, most people think our soul and spirit are the same. But our spirit is the part of us that is born again when we believe in Jesus. Our spirit is identical to Jesus. We have gifts of the Holy Spirit, such as love, joy, peace, long suffering, gentleness, goodness, faith, meekness and temperance (Galatians 5:22-23). Those things are always in our spirit—they have been there since the moment we were born again. In our spirit, we have the mind of Christ and an unction from the Holy Spirit and know all things (I Corinthians 2:16; 1 John 2:20).

Some people are going to read this and think, "That can't be true. I live in turmoil, I don't have any peace and I sure don't know all things." But it isn't our mind that knows everything; you can prove that. Many of us have searched the house looking for keys that were in our pocket the whole time. We are wrong more often than we like to admit and our natural minds obviously don't know everything there is to know. But in our spirits, we know all things. The mind is physical and we cannot perceive spiritual things by carnal means. The mind has to do with sense knowledge (what we see, taste, hear, smell, and feel). It is a part of our soul and the soul isn't made completely new when we are born again; our spirit is. In our spirit we are identical to Jesus. We have His power, anointing, wisdom, joy, peace, and love because the Holy Spirit is continually producing fruit in our spirit.

Our senses might be telling us that the world is caving in, but in our born-again spirit we have love, joy, and peace. The only way we can know what we have in our spirit is through the Word of God; it will divide between soul and spirit. The Word will show us who we are, no matter how we feel.

Finding God's will is really as simple as discerning whether our feelings are coming from the spirit or the flesh. It's simple, but it isn't easy because most of us don't know what is true in our spirit. We are dominated by what we can see, taste, hear, smell and feel. We don't think spiritually.

The Apostle John wrote that as Jesus is, so are we in this world (1 John 4:17). He didn't say that we will be like Jesus after we die and go to Heaven, he said *so are we in this world*. In our spirit we are identical to Jesus. I know that can be hard to believe, but it's true. When you look in the mirror, you may see zits, gray hair, and bulges, and think, "I sure don't look like Jesus." True, your physical body isn't like Jesus, but your spirit is identical to Him. As humans, we tend to assume that if our spirit is identical to Jesus, we will just know that to be true somehow. We think, "If I had love, I'd know it." Not true. The Bible says,

> *But the natural man receiveth not the things of the Spirit of God: for they are foolishness unto him: neither can he know them, because they are spiritually discerned.*

> *1 Corinthians 2:14*

Our little "peanut" brains don't know what happened to our spirit when we were born again, so our intellect doesn't know our spiritual identity. Some things can only be discerned spiritually. We can't look in a mirror and see our spirit. We can't feel around and sense our spirit. We can't try to feel with our emotions to see if we have joy in our spirit. Our spirit can't be felt by our physical senses. But the Word of God will show us what we don't intuitively know.

Jesus told His disciples, "the words that I speak unto you, they are spirit, and they are life" (John 6:63). The only way we can know what's going on in the spirit is through the Word. The Word shows us our spiritual identity. If we don't know the Word of God, we won't know who we are in our spirit. Our physical senses will dominate us, even though the whole time we have the same Spirit that raised Christ from the dead living inside of us (Romans 8:9 with Ephesians 1:19-20). The only way we are going to get what is in our spirit to flow out into our lives is by letting the Word of God speak to us and direct us.

It took me 20 years to understand everything I've just told you. This is powerful stuff. I guarantee you that understanding the makeup of the spirit, soul, and body will transform your life, but most people let this go right over their heads. They don't let the Word of God reveal to them who they are and what they have. People are begging God for results, instead of taking the Word of God and finding out their identity in Christ and using the Word like a sword.

I encourage you to get my teaching *Spirit, Soul & Body*. It goes into a lot more detail on this than I'm able to cover here and is foundational to understanding this.

You've Already Got It

Simon Peter, a servant and an apostle of Jesus Christ, to them that have obtained like precious faith with us through the righteousness of God and our Saviour Jesus Christ.

2 Peter 1:1

The Apostle Peter wrote this letter to people who have *like precious faith*. If you look that up in the Greek, it means "identical faith." This is written to people who have the identical faith that Peter had. If you say, "Oh, I could never claim that," then just go ahead and tear Second Peter out of your Bible, because that's who Peter is writing to. Everyone who has been born again has as much faith as Peter had. Peter walked on water (Matthew 14:29). He saw Dorcas raised from the dead (Acts 9:39-40). His shadow healed people as it passed over them (Acts 5:15). Peter did great miracles and you have the same faith he had!

Every person who has been born again and baptized in the Holy Spirit has enough power and anointing on the inside of them to raise the dead, walk on water, and have their shadow heal people. Every single one of us has this power. Somebody might say, "Yeah, I have faith, but it's just in little seed form. It hasn't grown yet." That's not true, your faith isn't growing. Faith is complete. You already have the fullness of faith on the inside. The problem is that you don't know what you have. You just need to renew your mind.

That the communication of thy faith may become effectual by the acknowledging of every good thing which is in you in Christ Jesus.

Philemon 1:6

The way your faith becomes effectual, or the way it begins to work, is by acknowledging what you already have. We don't need God to give us more faith. Every believer is given the same measure of faith at salvation (Romans 12:3; 2 Peter 1:1; Galatians

2:20). We need to use what God has already given us. Once, the disciples asked Jesus to increase their faith and He told them to use what they had (Luke 17:5-10). You don't need more faith; you need to realize that you already have faith. The Word of God shows us what we have. After introducing his letter by saying that he is writing it to those who have like precious faith, Peter wrote:

> *Grace and peace be multiplied unto you through the knowledge of God, and of Jesus our Lord, According as his divine power hath given unto us all things that pertain unto life and godliness, through the knowledge of him that hath called us to glory and virtue: Whereby are given unto us exceeding great and precious promises: that by these ye might be partakers of the divine nature, having escaped the corruption that is in the world through lust.*
>
> *2 Peter 1:2-4*

Grace and peace are multiplied through the knowledge of God and Jesus Christ. If you don't have knowledge, you aren't going to have peace. It doesn't matter how much you pray. You can have people pray for you until they rub all the hair off the top of your head, but you still won't have God's peace until you renew your mind. You can't operate contrary to your dominant thoughts. If you are focused on the problems you have and all that is going wrong in the world, you won't have peace. God keeps you in perfect peace when you keep your mind focused on Jesus (Isaiah 26:3).

Notice that the scripture says God *has* given us *all things* according to the knowledge of Him. We receive all the fullness of God through salvation. We experience this fullness by renewing our minds with the Word of God. In a sense, any problems we have in life are knowledge problems. Peace, healing, and direction all come through the knowledge of God that is revealed in His Word. We just need to know who we are and what we have in our spirits.

Jesus said that He came to give us life and to give it abundantly (John 10:10). He came to give us a life that is full of blessings. He proved this by going around healing everyone who was oppressed by the devil (Acts 10:38). Everything that it takes to have an abundant life comes through knowing God: healing, joy, peace, prosperity, abundance, vision, and every blessing.

The Word of God is the knowledge of God and everything we need comes through it. But the promise of everything coming through the knowledge of God assumes that we are going to act on the knowledge we have. Faith without works is dead (James 2:20). Prosperity, for instance, comes when we know what the Word says and act on that knowledge. Likewise, we have health in our bodies when we know that Jesus provided healing on the cross and take the steps to receive what the Lord has already provided. But if we don't act on what we know, we can miss out on the prosperity and healing God desires us to possess.

No problem exists that is bigger than God's supply. Whatever problem we might have, God can handle it. We just need to get away from being pressed into thinking the way the world thinks and renew our minds to the truth that nothing is impossible for God! We have to stop believing who the world says we are and find out who God says we are. We will find our spiritual identity in God's Word.

A Lamp Unto Your Feet

The longest chapter in the Bible is Psalm 119 and every verse of that psalm is about the importance of the Word of God. A lot of different phrases are used to describe the Word, like the law of the Lord or the statutes of the Lord, but they all refer to the Word of God.

Wherewithal shall a young man cleanse his way? By taking heed thereto according to thy word.

Psalm 119:9

When the Lord first touched my life back in 1968, I knew that Christians were supposed to walk in power and victory. I knew there was more to the Christian life than I had ever seen or heard, but I didn't know how to get from where I was to where I thought I should be. One night as I was kneeling at my bed praying, I opened my eyes and saw my Bible lying on my bed and heard the Lord say to me, *"If you put My Word in your heart, it will teach you everything you need to know."* My problem was immediately solved. I began to pour myself into the Bible and renew my mind by studying the Word.

I have more understanding than all my teachers: for thy testimonies are my meditation.

Psalm 119:99

The Word of God will give you understanding. Meditate on the Word day and night and it will make your way prosperous—then you will have good success (Joshua 1:8). Everybody wants to be prosperous and have good success, but we want to do it without meditating in the Word day and night because that might interfere with our TV schedule or our hobbies. Although Christians tend to value a lot of unimportant things above the Word, God still loves us. He isn't mad at us. We can go to heaven without knowing the Word of God well. Actually, we can get to heaven quicker that way because we won't be able to receive our healing. We will die prematurely. But if we want to live a victorious life and if we want understanding, we have to meditate on the Word.

Thy word is a lamp unto my feet, and a light unto my path.

Psalm 119:105

God directs our steps but He doesn't show us the end of the path from the beginning. He gives us just enough light to know where to go next—He doesn't show us step one through one hundred all at once. If He showed us everything all at once, it might overwhelm us or we might try to rush ahead of God and take a shortcut to the end. He only shows us one step at a time because He loves us.

I have people come to me all the time who know that God wants them to attend Charis Bible College, but they hesitate because they can't see how everything is going to work out. They are trying to see the end from the beginning. I remember one guy coming into my office who said he was certain that God had told him to go to Charis, but then he started telling me all the reasons he thought it wouldn't work out. He told me about his job, his girlfriend, and the opinions of his parents and pastor. When he was finished, he said, "So, what do you think?" I said, "You lost me the moment you said God told you to do it. If God told you to do it then forget all the rest." It's really pretty simple: if God tells you to do something—do it!

When God Almighty, who has a universe to run, takes the time to talk to you and tell you to do something, why would you try to reason it all out in order to decide whether you're going to do it or not? Something is seriously wrong with that approach. If that's the way you think, you aren't absolutely convinced that God is working for your best interest. God's plans for you are better than your plans for yourself. When the Lord tells you to do something, just do it!

I would rather step out on what I think God is telling me to do and be wrong than not do what He is telling me to because I want to play it safe. Then what would I say when I finally stood before God, "Lord, didn't You see all of the potential problems with Your plan?" God knows what He is doing and the challenges we will face. I don't want any of the miracles that God has put on the inside of me still there when I leave this world. I want to get them all out. I want to go for it!

Waiting for God to show us the whole picture before we step out is a bad plan; it isn't going to happen. God shows us His will in steps and stages. If we are out in pitch-black darkness, a lamp isn't going to illuminate something a hundred yards down the road. But it will show us the next step. That is exactly the way the Word works. As we read God's Word, He will tell us something and then we act on it. After we step into what God has said, we will be able to see the next step, and the next step, and so on.

Seed, Time, and Harvest

So is the kingdom of God, as if a man should cast seed into the ground; And should sleep, and rise night and day, and the seed should spring and grow up, he knoweth not how. For the earth bringeth forth fruit of herself; first the blade, then the ear, after that the full corn in the ear. But when the fruit is brought forth, immediately he putteth in the sickle, because the harvest is come.

Mark 4:26-29

Seeds need time to grow. They don't immediately sprout into fruit bearing plants. It's a process: first the blade, then the ear of corn buds, and later the full fruit of corn appears. The will of God comes in the same way: step by step. Understanding this principle will really help you.

I had a man come to me one time and show me his plans for a youth ministry project in our town. He saw a need for the youth so his plan was to buy an abandoned Kmart building for two million dollars, put another two million dollars into it, and start a youth center. He showed me all of the statistics, and he was right, we did need a youth center. So I asked him,

"Have you ever taught a Bible study?"

"No."

"Have you ever worked in a youth group?"

"No."

"Have you ever dealt with youth?"

"No."

He had never done any ministry work. I said, "It's a great idea, but it won't work for you."

"Why not?" he asked. Then he tried to justify his plans by the need.

I said, "It's first the blade, then the ear, and then the full corn in the ear. You have never been used a little bit so you aren't going to be used a lot."

God's will for your life doesn't come to pass immediately. For you to go from zero to a thousand miles an hour instantly isn't acceleration, it's a *wreck*. It takes time to build up speed. In the same way, there is a growth process involved in finding, following, and fulfilling God's will for your life. After you have been following God's leading for a while, maybe you will begin to see a bigger picture—but you won't get it all at once.

Do One Thing

…this one thing I do, forgetting those things which are behind, and reaching forth unto those things which are before, I press toward the mark for the prize of the high calling of God in Christ Jesus.

Philippians 3:13-14

The strength of a person lies in his or her focus. Like a laser, focus loses its power when it's diffused. If you want a laser to cut through metal, it has to be focused into a pinpoint. Paul said, "this *one* thing I do," and that's the reason he turned the world right-side up. You have to be focused if you want to really accomplish something.

The way to kill a man's vision is to give him two visions. Anyone who allows his attention to be spread around is as useless as a diffused laser. He will be distracted with the things of this world and his understanding will be darkened. Walking in the ways of the world hinders spiritual understanding, therefore our society is not conducive to knowing God. An ungodly, anti-Christian society promotes values and a way of life contrary to what God desires for us.

Sadly, a lot of Christians are plugged into the world and their hearts are divided, their understanding is darkened, and they are alienated from the life of God. Many believers are ignorant of the truth of God's Word because they spend five hours a day watching junk on TV. They read a little devotional for five minutes and think they have spent sufficient time in the Word. Trying to build a relationship with God on scraps of discarded time is not going to bring you to the center of His will. You have to make fellowship with God and reading His Word a priority.

> *The law of the LORD is perfect, converting the soul: the testimony of the LORD is sure, making wise the simple. The statutes of the LORD are right, rejoicing the heart: the commandment of the LORD is pure, enlightening the eyes.*

> *Psalm 19:7–8*

The Word of God is perfect and shows us the way back to God when we lose our way. If you have made some mistakes or have been discouraged or hurt, the Word of God will convert your soul. It will restore your joy and your faith. The soul is the mental and emotional part of you that can experience turmoil, but your born-again spirit is perfect and the Word will remind you of your true identity.

God's Word will make you wise; it will enlighten your eyes. This scripture isn't talking about your physical eyes. It's talking about the ability to see with your heart: to see by faith and perceive spiritual things that your physical eyes can't see. The Word of God will open your heart to know things that you can't know by your five senses.

The Word is God is the answer for any and every problem you might have. The Bible doesn't contain man's wisdom; it contains God's wisdom for man. It's a book from God that contains everything you need for life and godliness. I believe the King James translation is the best version available, but if you can't handle the "thee's" and "thou's" then get a translation you enjoy reading. Getting into the Word and learning God's way of thinking is the path to finding His will for your life.

Finding God's will for your life will give you a clear purpose and keep you from getting sidetracked by the challenges you face. It's much easier to persevere through hard times when you know you are going in the right direction. Knowing that you are doing what God created you to do will give you strength to weather the storms of life.

God has never made a piece of junk. He has never made a failure. Every person born into this world was created by God for a special purpose. Everyone has the potential of becoming something beautiful. Being in the center of God's will brings a sense of fulfillment. The relationship you form with God will spill over into your life and bless the people around you. The best part is that God's will isn't hard to find—He wants you to know it! But you have to go through the narrow gate of making yourself a living sacrifice. Once you make the commitment to find God's will, you will see Him begin to move in your life and awesome things will start to happen.

Chapter 6

Delight Yourself in the Lord

God has a specific plan for every person. It's not hard to find His will for our lives because He told us not to be ignorant but understand what the will of God is (Ephesians 5:17). The Lord wants us to know His will for our lives and it's absolutely essential for us to find it. We won't find God's will accidentally; we have to seek to find it (Matthew 7:7). Knowing God's will for our lives will allow us to set goals and help us persevere through difficulties. Finding God's will is essential, but it's only the starting point. There's a big difference between *finding* God's will and *following* it. After we discover what God's will for our life is, we have to purposely seek after it. We can't depend on fate to somehow make it happen.

I am going to discuss several things that will help you follow God's leading after you have found His will for your life. What I'm going to share is really simple, but it's dependent upon you continuing to make yourself a living sacrifice and renewing your mind with the Word of God (as we discussed earlier in this book). You never move beyond those first requirements. You can't make yourself a living sacrifice and renew your mind one time and never think about it again. Following and fulfilling God's will build upon the things we have already discussed. If you are doing those things then this simple, but profound, passage of scripture will help you:

> Trust in the LORD, and do good; so shalt thou dwell in the land, and verily thou shalt be fed. Delight thyself also in the LORD; and he shall give thee the desires of thine heart. Commit thy way unto the LORD; trust also in him; and he shall bring it to pass.
>
> Psalm 37:3-5

When we delight ourselves in the Lord, He puts His desires in our heart. Some people misinterpret this scripture to mean that God will give them whatever they want: a million dollar house, a luxury car, a particular job, a promotion, or whatever. But this is not a free pass to get our hands on anything our flesh craves. Some people desire another person's spouse. God is not going to help them fulfill desires like that. As we seek the Lord with our whole heart, He will change our hearts to desire godly things. Suddenly, the ungodly things we were doing before we gave our lives to the Lord won't appeal to us any longer. A lot of people experience this after they are born again.

The Hebrew word that was translated *delight* in this verse literally means, "to be soft or pliable." It's speaking about having a sensitive heart towards the Lord. So, to delight in the Lord means to commit our lives to Him, to the degree that we are seeking His will and ways. It's putting Him first. *If* we do these things, God will order the desires of our heart. But that's a big *"if."* I emphasize "if" because even though being totally committed to God is our normal Christian duty (Romans 12:1), it's uncommon to see this. Christians are by no means perfect, but we should desire to seek God with our whole heart.

We all have to deal with our carnal nature and cope with the fact that we live in a sinful world and have thoughts and emotions that can lead us astray. I'm not saying that we have to live perfectly in order to be totally committed to God, but we should have a desire to live more for God than for ourselves. When we try to live for God, which is what it means to delight ourselves in the Lord, then God will put His desires in our heart. It's pretty simple.

One of the most common ways God leads us is by the desires of our heart. Before we can trust our desires, we need to make sure that we're really delighting in the Lord. It isn't hard to tell if we are putting God first, all we have to do is be honest with ourselves. Proverbs says that the heart knows its own bitterness (Proverbs 14:10). If God isn't first in our lives, we can't depend on being led by the desires of our heart; we will lust after things that aren't godly. The desires of our heart will not be the same as God's will for us, unless we're delighting in Him.

Be Spiritually Minded

I was brought up in a legalistic church. When they taught on finding God's will, they actually said, "Whatever you want to do, do the exact opposite and that will be God." I don't recommend following that advice. But this is true for carnal Christians, people who make satisfying their own needs the greatest priority in their lives. The Bible says, "the carnal mind is enmity against God: for it is not subject to the law of God, neither indeed can be" (Romans 8:6). So it's true that people who don't pursue a relationship with God after they are born again can't trust their desires. Anyone who is just waiting on heaven might be saved, but they are stuck living by their carnal nature. Those believers can't trust the desires of their heart to be godly.

Everyone who is truly committed to God can be led by the desires of their heart. I could tell you a hundred stories from my life that show how God has led me in the best decisions I have ever made, just by using the simple principle of being led by my desires. For instance, I never wanted a Bible school. A lot of people asked me to start one, but I never wanted to, largely because I had met too many Bible school graduates who really annoyed me. They thought they were better than other Christians because they could quote Scripture. But they didn't have a better relationship with God nor did they love God more than the people they looked down on. I didn't want to be associated with something like that, so I had no desire to start a Bible school, even though I have always had a strong desire to disciple people.

In the summer of 1993, I was in the UK and heard a man say that if you aren't training up people to do what God has shown you, you're a failure. It doesn't matter if you reach a hundred thousand people for Christ. Our time on earth is limited, so unless you can take what is in you and reproduce it in other people, then ultimately, you have failed. Christians are supposed to make disciples, not converts.

I knew those things were true so it stirred something in me when I heard someone else preach about it. I thought, *God, how can I equip believers to help them start walking in the abundant life You have made available?* The Lord answered me, "A Bible school." God showed me a new way to approach Bible school and in one church service, the desires of my heart changed completely. I went from being totally opposed to having a Bible school to being really excited about the idea.

Charis Bible College grew from the desire God planted in my heart that day. The core of this program is two years of instruction, focusing on building a relationship with God while increasing ones scriptural knowledge. Today, we have several campuses in the United States and multiple extension colleges around the world. Charis Bible College graduates are teaching and preaching in the United States, as well as doing great missionary work in Russia, Africa, India, South America, and other countries all over the globe.

I'm really excited about the future of the school and the impact graduates will make for the kingdom of God. And all of this began when God simply changed the desires of my heart. He didn't speak to me in an audible voice; I didn't have it confirmed by three goose bumps and a prophecy. God just led me by changing my desires.

I started on television in the same way. It was different in the aspect that I always knew I would be on television one day. I was very aware that television was a huge step. The expense associated with television is much more than the radio I had been doing for decades. I knew if God wasn't in this, I could destroy the foothold I had worked decades to secure. Although I knew television was in my future, I wasn't excited about taking that step.

In the summer of 1998 as I was thinking about where our ministry was, I realized that at the rate we were growing, it would take 150 years for us to reach all of America with the truths God had shown me—forget about trying to reach the rest of the world! I said, "God, You know this isn't working. What do we have to do?" All of a sudden I thought, *Television.* And the most amazing part was that I had a desire to do it.

Right then, I drew a picture of the set that we ended up using for the first twelve years of our TV ministry. I saw what the program was going to look like. I knew I wasn't going to be wearing a three piece suit, marching back and forth in front of a large crowd, and wiping the sweat from my brow as I preached. I saw how God wanted *me* to do it, so I became excited about television. It was a one hundred and eighty degree turn from where I was before God changed my desires.

Whenever my desires change suddenly like that and I think it might be God leading me in a new direction, especially if the potential consequences are big, I make sure that I am delighting myself in the Lord with all of my heart. When I'm not sure, I fast, turn off television, get away from other people, and try to focus my mind on God as best as I can. I worship, pray, study the Word, and seek God stronger than I have been. In other words, I seek God with my whole heart.

As I seek God, the desire in my heart either increases or decreases. If the desire gets smaller, I conclude that it was probably a carnal desire of my flesh. But if the desire keeps getting stronger and I start getting further revelation as I seek God with all of my heart, I know God is leading me. I have based my life on the knowledge that when I am seeking God and delighting myself in the Lord, He puts His desires in my heart. Some of the biggest decisions of my life were based on nothing more than seeking God first and following the desires in my heart.

I promise you that this principle works. God is doing awesome things for us. I am absolutely confident that I am on the right path. I haven't arrived, but praise God, I've left. I'm moving in the right direction. I know I'm where God wants me to be. This is how you get there: put God first in your life and then follow the desires of your heart. Unfortunately, most people do not follow their heart. They let conventional wisdom dominate them. They allow circumstances and money to dictate their course in life instead of following the desires of their heart.

But What About ...?

Forget your fears and phobias about what you can or cannot do. For a moment, forget all of your financial obligations and how far away from retirement you are. Remove every restriction that is holding you back. Now, what do you want to do? Are you doing what you really want to be doing with your life?

The majority of people to whom I have asked this question say they are not doing what they really want to do. Life is too short for that. I tell people if they aren't living on the edge, they are taking up too much space. You need to be out there. You need to be doing something. Life isn't a dress rehearsal. You don't get a second shot at life. Is anybody going to miss you when you're gone? Have you made a difference? If you are truly putting God first, then your desires are telling you what you were born to do. Your heart knows what your purpose in life is.

We preach a lot on vision at Charis Bible College, therefore I've had students come to me when it gets close to the end of school and say, "I still don't know what God wants me to do. I've prayed but I haven't heard a thing." So I sit down with them and tell them what I have just told you: forget about money for right now, act like you have billions of dollars and money is not even an issue; forget about what your relatives and friends are saying; forget about past experiences that have made you feel like a failure—forget about all of that stuff. If there were no restrictions on you, what would you want to do?

Sometimes people aren't sure. But everybody, I mean *everybody*, has desires on the inside of them. Every person I have ever counseled with had a dream of some kind. Once they got over all of their phobias and out of the mindset of trying to do what everyone else expected them to do, they started to express their dreams. I have talked to dozens, maybe hundreds of people, who really did have a Word from God, but they didn't trust their own desires. They thought the desire was coming from them so they dismissed it. Most of us would rather have an angel appear to us— or a burning bush speak to us and tell us what to do.

I have never heard the audible voice of God. I'm not saying God doesn't speak to people in a voice that is heard like conversation, but it's not how He typically communicates with us. Usually, hearing from God is as simple as putting God first in your life, seeking Him with your whole heart, and following the desires of your heart. Again, you have to check those desires against the Word of God. The desire to rob a bank or commit some other sin obviously doesn't come from God. However, if the desire of your heart increases the more you seek God and pray, you need to follow it.

I think a lot of people have let life beat the dreams out of them. They have been disappointed so many times, they don't want to put themselves out on a limb and risk being disappointed again. Other people feel like dreaming is for kids so they put their dreams on a shelf in order to pursue what the world values. But God didn't create us to trudge through life just trying to make ends meet. Life is meant to be exciting. We are meant to know the joy of feeling like our life is making a difference.

Serving God is not boring. If you're bored, you haven't found God's will for your life. Following God's will is like riding a roller coaster: there's excitement at every curve. You will face challenges and be stretched. Not everyone is supposed to be in full-time ministry, trying to reach millions of people, but everyone should be excited about the future and what they are doing. God didn't create any of us to just occupy space.

The Body of Christ

When I was in Lamar, Colorado, I had a Bible study. There were seven sisters who attended this particular Bible study. They were all fanatical about God. One time, one of the sister's toddler pulled a motorcycle on top of himself and it crushed his chest. The sister just pushed his chest back into its normal shape and prayed over him for about thirty minutes. She commanded him to live and he came back to life.

Another time, the mother of these seven sisters died so they prayed over her and she was raised from the dead. Then their mother stood up, walked two miles into town, bought groceries, and came back. These sisters aren't on television, they aren't even preachers, but they are walking in the supernatural power of God. Their town knows who they are and people have been born again because of their testimony. They are making a difference. Their lives count!

God doesn't want everybody to be a full-time preacher or teacher, but He wants us all to be ministers of His love. He wants all of us to live a life that makes an impact for the kingdom of God. Our lives should count. We should be part of a church where we can be involved in something bigger than ourselves. The American dream of building our own personal empire is not God's dream. God wants our lives to impact others in a positive way.

Nobody lies on their death bed and says, "Oh, I wish I had owned a bigger house and nicer cars. I wish I had more diamonds and jewels." The regrets people have at the end of their lives involve relationship failures. People regret that their lives didn't make a bigger impact, because life is all about relationships. God is in the people business. Whatever God's purpose for your life is, somehow or another, it is going to relate to changing people.

One of my employees had a friend who believed beyond any shadow of a doubt that God led him into the garbage collecting business. He rightly pointed out that somebody has to collect the garbage; it would be unhealthy if they didn't. This guy would straighten up everyone's garbage can and always leave things nice and tidy. He took pride in what he did and used collecting garbage as an opportunity to witness to the love of God. He felt fulfilled because every day he had the opportunity to show somebody the kindness of God or tell somebody about the Lord. Every believer has that same supernatural love and power of God. No matter what God has called you to do, you can use His love and power to impact the lives around you.

Get Out of the Boat

God will lead you in multiple ways, but probably the number one way you learn how to follow God's will is simply by putting Him first and following the desires He puts in your heart. When you delight yourself in the Lord, He changes the desires of your heart to align with your purpose. You can trust those desires. This is how God will lead you most of the time. He is not likely to speak to you in an audible voice or appear to you in a visible form. That's why it takes faith to follow God's leading.

> *... without faith it is impossible to please him: for he that cometh to God must believe that he is, and that he is a rewarder of them that diligently seek him.*
>
> *Hebrews 11:6*

God delights in revealing Himself in subtle ways. Jesus could have come to earth on a 747 jet and landed in Jerusalem, but He chose to come meekly instead. Joseph had to take it by faith that Mary had gotten pregnant by the Holy Spirit and not through a natural human relationship. When Jesus rose from the dead, He could have hovered over Jerusalem to prove to everyone who crucified Him that He was alive again. Instead, after Jesus rose from the dead, He only appeared to people who already believed in Him. Jesus could have forced people to recognize His resurrection, but that's not how God does things. He wants people to believe by faith. He doesn't force His will on anybody.

If you are putting God first, then He has been trying to lead you by putting His desires in your heart. But you have to get out of the boat. You have to take a step and get out on the water. Be bold enough to step out and follow the desires of your heart. Your life will take on meaning; it will be exciting! You will make an impact in the lives of others. It will be worth the risk of getting out of your comfort zone.

You might be thinking, "I'm afraid I'll sink. I should just stay in the boat." When Peter stepped out of the boat to walk toward Jesus on the sea (Matthew 14:25-33), the boat was already full of water. They were all about to drown. There was very little difference between being *in* the boat and being *out* of the boat. Many believers are afraid of stepping out and following God's leading, yet they are miserable. They are stuck in the same rut as everyone else—work, television, and sleep—but they won't do anything to change. What do you have to lose? At least when you are out of the boat, you will be following God. You'll be taking a chance. In order to walk on water, you have to get out of the boat!

You need to use wisdom in order to do what God leads you to do in His timing. Don't just sit still and wait for it to happen on its own. Do something. Take a step. When someone feels led to come to Charis Bible College but they can't see how it is going to work out, I tell them to put down the registration fee and see what happens. It's a step. Once you get a boat moving, even if it is barely moving, the rudder can change its course. But if the boat is motionless, you can flip the rudder 360 degrees and never change direction. You have to do something in order for God to steer you. If you aren't totally sure, don't go full-steam ahead—move slowly. Just start doing something.

The book of Second Kings tells the story of four lepers who sat at the entrance to the besieged city of Samaria. Inside the city there was famine; the citizens were eating cow dung and even their own children, in some cases. The enemy had the city surrounded and their supplies were cut off. The lepers said,

> *Why sit we here until we die? If we say, We will enter into the city, then the famine is in the city, and we shall die there: and if we sit still here, we die also. Now therefore come, and let us fall unto the host of the Syrians: if they save us alive, we shall live; and if they kill us, we shall but die.*

2 Kings 7:3-4

The lepers knew that heading down toward the enemy camp was dangerous but they realized they were going to die anyway. At least by taking a risk, they had a chance of surviving. So they went out to the camp of the Syrians. When they arrived, they discovered the Lord had already defeated the enemy. The entire camp was deserted and their food was still cooking on the fire. They found gold, silver, and raiment, and became instantly wealthy. After their discovery, the lepers returned to the city to share the good news of how the enemy had fled.

Those four lepers brought deliverance to the entire city of Samaria. They became heroes because somebody finally said, "How long am I going to sit here, until I die?" It's better to take a step of faith and fail than to sit around doing nothing and call it success. God can bless you doing the wrong thing because you are trying to move in faith—more than He can bless you doing nothing out of fear, which is unbelief. If God has put a desire in your heart, don't sit around waiting until you die, do something about it!

I hope you can feel the Holy Spirit trying to stir you up. You need to be stirred-up, if you aren't, you will settle to the bottom. God wants you to reach your full potential. When my life is over, I want to look back and say, "Father, thank You. I've run the race. I've finished the course (2 Timothy 4:7). I gave it everything I had." I don't want to reach the end of my life and say, "I wish I had done what was really in my heart." To the best of my ability, I'm doing what's in my heart. I want to encourage you to do the same. You won't ever arrive, but you need to leave the station.

It isn't enough just to find God's will. You have to begin to take steps to follow His leading. Being in the center of God's will brings a sense of satisfaction that you will never experience when you are out of His will. It doesn't matter if you love God and live a holy life. You still need to be where God wants you to be in order to experience the satisfaction and contentment that only comes from being in His will.

The main way God has directed me into the center of His will has been by the desires of my heart. As you seek God first in your life, He will put His desires in your heart, then it's up to you to act on your desires. You don't have to make an all-out charge toward what God is leading you to do if you aren't certain. Just take a few steps toward the desire in your heart. The Lord delights in faith, and when you begin to step out in faith, He will show Himself strong on your behalf (2 Chronicles 16:9).

Chapter 7

Timing and Preparation

Moses was a great man of God. He pursued God's will for his life with tremendous dedication, but he also made some major mistakes along the way. He caused himself, along with the entire Jewish nation, a lot of grief. Moses had a revelation of God's will for his life but he didn't have a clue how to fulfill it. As a result, he tried doing things his own way and caused a lot of problems. Moses is a prime example of why learning how to cooperate with God is a key element in following His leading.

When Moses was born, Pharaoh had given an order to kill all of the male children born to the Israelites (Exodus 1:15-16). During this time, the population of the Israelites was multiplying greatly and Pharaoh was afraid they would take over the land of Egypt, so he ordered the midwives to kill all the male children.

I find it interesting that every time in history when a dominant godly leader was about to come on the scene, such as Jesus or Moses, there was a move by the government to kill infants (Matthew 2:16). It's like Satan could tell that something was coming and he tried to stop it by killing the babies. In our own time, there have been over 50 million babies aborted since 1973 in the United States alone. In fact, abortion is the leading cause of death in America—it kills almost twice as many people annually as heart disease, while accounting for 39% of all deaths in America 2005.[1]

The sad part is that abortion is being promoted around the world as a solution to unwanted pregnancies. You just can't ignore the fact that there's a huge movement to kill infants. I believe it's because we are at the end time. Just as when Moses and Jesus were born, Satan is trying to prevent God from carrying out the final stages in His plan of redemption, but God always has a way to circumvent Satan's evil schemes.

God was able to preserve Moses through the time of infanticide in Egypt. His parents kept him for three months and when they couldn't hide him any longer, his mother put him in a basket daubed with pitch and let it drift down along the edge of the Nile River. Moses' sister watched from a distance to see what would happen. Pharaoh's daughter went down to the river to bathe, saw the basket among the rushes, and discovered Moses. She knew he had to be one of the Hebrew children so she took him and raised him as her own.

I love how God operates: Satan was trying to kill the Israelites' potential leader, using Pharaoh as his instrument—so God

---

[1] "Abortion Blackout; end abortion by 2020," http://www.abortionblack out.com/abortion-facts?page=2

sent the leader directly to Pharaoh to supply his upbringing, education, and training. God always has a way of getting His will accomplished.

> *And it came to pass in those days, when Moses was grown, that he went out unto his brethren, and looked on their burdens: and he spied an Egyptian smiting an Hebrew, one of his brethren. And he looked this way and that way, and when he saw that there was no man, he slew the Egyptian, and hid him in the sand. And when he went out the second day, behold, two men of the Hebrews strove together: and he said to him that did the wrong, Wherefore smitest thou thy fellow? And he said, Who made thee a prince and a judge over us? intendest thou to kill me, as thou killedst the Egyptian? And Moses feared, and said, Surely this thing is known. Now when Pharaoh heard this thing, he sought to slay Moses. But Moses fled from the face of Pharaoh, and dwelt in the land of Midian: and he sat down by a well.*
>
> *Exodus 2:11-15*

This small amount of information summarizes the first 40 years of Moses' life. I like the old movie *The Ten Commandments*, but it is totally inaccurate in a lot of its details. The movie seems to rely solely on the book of Exodus for its account of Moses' life, but to truly understand the story of Moses you need information that is only provided in the New Testament. Without that information, some inaccurate conclusions will be drawn. In the books of Acts and Hebrews, the Holy Spirit inspired the authors to write about

Moses and fill in the details that you don't get by reading the book of Exodus. The Bible is its own commentary—that's a good principle to remember.

The *Ten Commandments* portrays that Moses sort of fell into his destiny when he saw an Egyptian beating a Hebrew. Then out of a sense of right and wrong, he defended the Hebrew by killing the Egyptian. The movie conveys a common misconception that Moses didn't know that he was a Jew, however Scripture shows otherwise—Moses *did* know his heritage.

Stephen was the first Christian martyr. Right before he was stoned to death, he recounted Jewish history to the council to show that he wasn't against the Jewish faith. He started with Abraham and went on through the promises and prophecies that were given to the Jews about the coming of the Messiah. Stephen was speaking under the inspiration of the Holy Spirit and the things he said fill in the blanks to give us a better understanding of what actually happened to Moses. He said,

> *In which time Moses was born, and was exceeding fair, and nourished up in his father's house three months: And when he was cast out, Pharaoh's daughter took him up, and nourished him for her own son. And Moses was learned in all the wisdom of the Egyptians, and was mighty in words and in deeds. And when he was full forty years old, it came into his heart to visit his brethren the children of Israel.*
>
> *Acts 7:20-23*

This is the only place in the Bible where we learn that Moses was 40 years old when he killed the Egyptian. It says when he was 40 years old, *"it came into his heart to visit his brethren, the children of Israel."* This reflects what I taught about delighting in the Lord and God putting His desires in our heart. Moses knew he was a Jew. He saw the oppression of the Jews; he related to it. God put it in his heart to go and visit his brethren. Moses didn't find himself among the Jews accidentally when he saw the Hebrew man being beaten. It was in his heart to be there.

Timing Is Everything

And seeing one of them suffer wrong, he defended him, and avenged him that was oppressed, and smote the Egyptian: For he supposed his brethren would have understood how that God by his hand would deliver them: but they understood not.

Acts 7:24-25

This verse makes it crystal clear that Moses knew God had called him. He knew God had raised him up and put him in a position of leadership so he could bring deliverance to the Jews. Moses knew God's will for his life but thought that it was going to happen by killing an Egyptian. Moses thought the Jews would recognize how God had anointed him to rescue them and deliver them through his position in Pharaoh's household.

We don't know how long Moses had known God's will for his life, but he knew it. Even though Moses knew God was going to use him to deliver the Jews, he totally missed God's timing and plan for bringing it to pass. This is a critical piece of information for us. Finding out God's will for our life is absolutely imperative. But, if all we have is knowledge of God's will and aren't sensitive enough to be led by the Holy Spirit, we can blow the whole deal.

Moses blew it big time when he tried to bring God's will to pass in his own strength. His mistake cost him 40 years in the wilderness. It also cost the Jews 30 years of extra bondage, which God never intended. We know this because when God made the promise to Abraham, He prophesied that the children of Israel would be sojourners in a foreign land for 400 years (Genesis 15:13)—not 400 years of slavery in Egypt, but a total of 400 years from the time God made the promise. The Israelites were always strangers in the land because they didn't own the land they lived on. The Apostle Paul wrote that the law came 430 years after the promise (Galatians 3:17). The day Moses led the Israelites out of Egypt was the end of the 430 years (Exodus 12:40).

These calculations don't make you want to jump up, shout, and get all excited, but they are important. It was exactly 430 years from the time of God's prophesy to Abraham, until the children of Israel came out of the land of Egypt—yet God prophesied that it would be 400 years, leaving a 30 year discrepancy. We know that Moses spent 40 years in the wilderness after killing the Egyptian before he encountered God in the burning bush (Acts 7:30). So if you subtract the 40 years that Moses spent in the wilderness from the 430 years that it took for them to come out of the land of Egypt, they were only in the 390th year of the prophecy when Moses went out and killed the Egyptian and tried to bring God's will to pass. Moses was 10 years premature in trying to bring about what God had put in his heart.

God's will for your life involves His timing. You can't just take a Word from God, make a paragraph out of it, and do whatever you want to. God's plans can't be sped up. You can delay God's plan—Moses delayed it 40 years—but you can't make it happen any quicker than it's supposed to.

The Bible doesn't tell us exactly what was going on here, but I believe we can guess what Moses was thinking. He was a Jew who miraculously survived the infanticide of all male Jewish babies in Egypt, and he didn't eke out a living in some remote corner of the world—he grew up in Pharaoh's household! He was raised by Pharaoh's daughter. Moses was second or third in command over the entire Egyptian nation. Secular accounts say that he was a great general who conquered Ethiopia with the military might of Egypt. Moses was a powerful man who had a lot of influence in Egypt. It isn't hard to imagine Moses assuming that it would be his own position and power that would allow him to bring deliverance to the Israelites. But God doesn't rely upon the strength of men.

God wasn't going to deliver Israel in some way that would allow Moses to get all of the credit. It wasn't going to be Moses' position within the household of Pharaoh that gave Israel freedom. God was going to do it in a miraculous way so there would be no mistaking *Who* saved them.

Preparation Time is Never Wasted Time

A lot of people in the body of Christ take the same approach to God's will as Moses did. They may have stumbled upon God's will, but after they know what God wants them to do, they think, "Okay, God, I can handle it from here. You just get me introduced, put me on the stage, and I'll do the rest. Lord, what a wise choice you made in picking me. I can see Your wisdom." A lot of ministers approach God's will in the same way. God touched them but now they are trying to build God's kingdom in their own ability, using their own wisdom. This is causing tremendous problems in the body of Christ.

God is going to call you to do something that is absolutely beyond your natural ability. He wants to do things in a supernatural way so it testifies of His glory and people recognize His love for them. God uses people to do things beyond their ability so when others see it, they say, "Wow! That had to be God!" God uses the base things of the world, things that are despised, things that are nothing, so no flesh will glory in His presence and say, "Look what I did." (1 Corithians 1:26-30.)

God is going to call you to do something that is beyond yourself so you will rely on His power. Then when people see God's power, they will give Him the glory. God wanted to do something supernatural through Moses, but Moses initially made the mistake of trying to get it done on his own. We don't know for sure whether Moses knew of the prophecy that said Israel would be delivered after 400 years, but I suspect he did—the Jews were very diligent in passing on their history. I believe Moses knew that he was ten years premature.

We are just as eager today to get things done instead of waiting around. We use reasoning to justify our impatience—in violation of Scripture—because it's convenient. The Bible teaches us not to put a novice into a position of leadership (1 Timothy 3:6), yet we regularly make newly born-again movie stars, athletes, and politicians the star representatives of Christianity. We do this in order to take advantage of their popularity. We think we can use their clout to promote the Gospel. We don't want to wait because they might lose their stature during the time it takes them to mature. Such impatience can backfire when the new believer gets lifted up in pride or falls into public scandal because of his or her immaturity.

Moses could have used similar logic. Maybe he observed all of the Jews dying under the harsh conditions in Egypt—say it was 100,000 people a year—and he thought, "God, I know it's still ten years before the prophecy will come to pass, but if I don't do something now, one million people are going to die before You deliver them from Egypt." It's the same logic we use when we let our needs and circumstances motivate us to do things contrary to how God has instructed us. The problem with this logic is that Moses' impatience actually delayed the Israelites' deliverance 30 years, which means that an extra three million people died unnecessarily. God would have brought them out from slavery 30 years earlier if Moses had followed His timing.

This is exactly how we act today. For instance, someone discovers that God has called them to be an evangelist, but they think, "I can't wait, people are dying and going to Hell. I can't take time to go to Bible school or get prepared. I have to get out and start reaching people right now." What he isn't considering is how many people might be turned off from the Lord because he got out there in his own strength and made a mess of things. We can't count how many people will be turned away from God if we crash and become a negative statistic. There is a right way, and a wrong way, to go about accomplishing God's will.

God revealed His will to Moses ten years before he was supposed to deliver the Jews from Egypt, in order to prepare him for what was ahead. From the time Samuel anointed David to be king until he actually became king was a minimum of 13 years. The Apostle Paul spent 14 years preparing for his ministry. If you go through the Bible and study the lives of the main characters, you will see that ten years would have been the least amount of time anybody spent in preparation to be used by God in a major way! I believe if Moses had waited another ten years, he could have prepared in the luxury of Pharaoh's palace, without all the hardships in the wilderness. God didn't send Moses into the desert. Moses went into the wilderness for 40 years because he committed murder, trying to bring God's will to pass in his own strength.

Do It God's Way

The moment most people get any kind of direction from God, *zoom*—they are gone. They don't wait for instructions. It's just as important to understand God's plan for accomplishing His will as it is to discover what His will is. You need the wisdom of God to be able to accomplish His will. He may want you to do something in a way that is totally different from anything you have ever seen before. Too many people in the body of Christ are just copying what other preachers are doing. One church builds a successful ministry by sending buses into poor neighborhoods to give free rides, so everybody starts a "bus ministry." Another pastor starts a "seeker-friendly" church, so everyone goes to a conference to learn how to mimic that approach. God has a plan for *you* and He can tell *you* what to do. You will only find out what God is leading you to do through a personal relationship with Him.

God's way of doing things is different than our way. For instance, it makes sense from a worldly perspective to hoard money when you are in need, but hoarding is wrong. The Bible teaches us to give and riches will be given unto us. God just does things differently than we do (Isaiah 55:8-9).

Jesus came upon Peter, James, and John one morning after they had been toiling all night in their fishing boats and hadn't caught a thing (Luke 5). They were gathering up their gear and getting ready to quit. Jesus told them to launch out into the deep and let down their nets one more time. Peter replied, "Master, we have toiled all night and have taken nothing: nevertheless at thy word I will let down the net." They did the same thing they had been doing the entire previous night, but this time they did it with God's direction and every fish in the Sea of Galilee tried to jump into their net! They caught so many fish that the net broke.

Notice that Jesus told them to let down their *nets*, plural, but they only let down *one* net. They obeyed, but they didn't *totally* obey. They halfway obeyed because they weren't expecting much. So instead of letting down several nets, they only let down one. The single net they put into the sea couldn't contain all of the fish that God had for them, so it broke. Many of the fish must have escaped. Think of the haul they would have had if they had completely obeyed Jesus by putting down multiple nets.

As you allow God to lead you, you might feel led to do something you have already done in the past. Don't immediately think, "Oh, I've already tried this and it didn't work." Maybe it didn't work because you were trying to do it on your own, instead of at God's command. You might do the exact same thing you did before and get totally different results, because this time you would be doing it under God's anointing and leadership.

God doesn't have a "one-size-fits-all" approach for building His kingdom. Our personal relationship with Jesus allows Him to guide us individually. It is one of the things that sets Christianity apart from every other religion on the face of the earth. Other religions have systems and rules and regulations, but we have a personal relationship. Every believer is God-possessed. Jesus lives on the inside of us. The Holy Spirit comes and fills us. He will talk to us, teach us, and guide us. He doesn't only speak to preachers and full-time ministers; the Holy Spirit is available to every born-again believer.

Moses had a word from God, but he didn't follow God's timing. Moses did what most of us would have done: he went out on his own and blew it. *We are not capable of representing God and accomplishing His plans in our own strength and ability.* The Lord didn't create us to be wound up like a toy robot, so He could release us to go off on our own speed and energy. We have to be God dependant. One of my favorite scriptures is, "O LORD, I know that the way of man is not in himself: it is not in man that walketh to direct his steps" (Jeremiah 10:23). We not only need to find God's will; we need to find His timing and plan for accomplishing it—which is only going to come through a relationship with the Lord that is build upon prayer and studying the Word.

Chapter 8

It Takes Effort

Moses blew it when he killed the Egyptian but he recovered and eventually went on to accomplish God's will. He spent 40 years in the wilderness praying and asking God for another chance. He knew God had a plan for his life. He never stopped seeking after God and trying to fulfill his purpose. Moses was actively looking for God, so when he saw a bush that was burning but wasn't being consumed by the flames, he turned aside to investigate.

> *Now Moses kept the flock of Jethro his father in law, the priest of Midian: and he led the flock to the backside of the desert, and came to the mountain of God, even to Horeb. And the angel of the Lord appeared unto him in a flame of fire out of the midst of a bush: and he looked, and, behold, the bush burned with fire, and the bush was not consumed. And Moses said, I will now turn aside, and see this great sight, why the bush is not burnt.*

> *Exodus 3:1–4*

It was only after Moses turned aside to check things out that the voice of God came to him. Moses could have walked right by the burning bush. He could have been focused on how far he had to travel with the flock. He could have been anxious to get them water by a certain time. I'm sure he was busy, but he was still looking for God. Then when he saw something abnormal, he stopped to investigate.

This same thing happened to the disciples when they were in the boat, struggling to survive a storm in the middle of the Sea of Galilee. Jesus came walking to them on the water. The scripture says He would have passed them by (Mark 6:48). Jesus was there to save His disciples. He wasn't out on the lake for a stroll and it just so happened that He walked close to their boat. No, Jesus was there to help them. But this is how God operates: He delights in faith. We have to be looking for Him.

God makes His presence known but He isn't going to force anyone to pay attention. God doesn't come into our life and *make* us follow him. To Moses' credit, he persevered in looking for God. He believed that God was still going to use him (Hebrews 11:27). If Moses had not turned aside to inspect the burning bush, it's very possible God wouldn't have spoken to him.

It's our hard-heartedness that makes us so insensitive to God. He isn't hard to find, it's just that most of us are looking in the wrong places. We are occupied with the wrong things. The Bible says when we seek, we find. We can't say, "God, if You can reach me in the next five minutes before my favorite TV program comes on I'll serve you for the rest of my life." God doesn't work on our timetable. We have to seek Him with all of our heart (Jeremiah 29:13), expecting to see Him intervene.

And he said, Draw not nigh hither: put off thy shoes from off thy feet, for the place whereon thou standest is holy ground. Moreover he said, I am the God of thy father, the God of Abraham, the God of Isaac, and the God of Jacob. And Moses hid his face; for he was afraid to look upon God.

Exodus 3:5-6

The Lord went on to tell Moses that He was sending him down to Egypt to bring the Jews out. Moses replied, "Who am I, that I should go unto Pharaoh, and that I should bring forth the children of Israel out of Egypt?" (Exodus 3:11)

Moses responded to God by saying, "I can't talk. I'm not wise. I'm not learned. They won't listen to me." Yet Moses was educated in all of the wisdom of the Egyptians and was mighty in word and deed (Acts 7:22). The Egyptians were a very advanced society, so Moses wasn't a fool. He was wise. Moses was just like you and I when we say we can't do something God asks us to do. The truth is, we can do it, but we get intimidated or overwhelmed so we start saying that we can't. With God's help and His anointing, we can do anything He asks us to (Philippians 4:13).

This attitude is in stark contrast to Moses' self-confidence 40 years earlier. It took a few decades in the wilderness for Moses to come to the end of himself. As long as you are sufficient in your-self, trusting in yourself, then you are going to have a hard time trusting God. You won't find the beginning of God until you get to the end of yourself. Moses was a different person with a different outlook. He was no longer second in command over all of Egypt—he was working for his father-in-law, herding sheep in the desert. Moses had lost the arrogance and self-will from his days as a prince of the world.

The Rod of God

Moses was looking for an opportunity to get back and fulfill God's will, yet he had lost his self-confidence. He still believed God was going to use him but he had to realize he couldn't do it on his own. Moses told the Lord he couldn't do what He was asking and that the people wouldn't believe him.

> *And the LORD said unto him, What is that in thine hand? And he said, A rod. And he said, Cast it on the ground. And he cast it on the ground, and it became a serpent; and Moses fled from before it. And the LORD said unto Moses, Put forth thine hand, and take it by the tail. And he put forth his hand, and caught it, and it became a rod in his hand.*
>
> *Exodus 4:2-3*

Moses fled from the snake in fear. God called him back and told him to pick the snake up by the tail. Picking up a serpent by the tail means you have no control. In order to control a snake you have to grab it right behind the jaws, otherwise it can turn and bite you. Moses was putting his life on the line by grabbing the tail of a venomous snake, which shows that he was willing to risk death in order to obey God.

Moses had been in "Bush University" for 40 years and this was his final exam. Would he pass or fail? When God told Moses to pick up the snake by the tail, He was saying, "Show Me that you are willing to do it My way." This would show that he was no longer dependent on his own understanding. Moses picked up the snake by the tail, thinking it was going to kill him, but instead the snake turned back into a stick. After all he had been through, Moses finally understood that God's way was better.

The Lord has to accomplish this same thing in everyone. All of us tend to want to control our own lives. We don't like being told what to do—not even by God. It's a characteristic of fallen human beings to want to do things our own way. In the process of finding God's will and trying to fulfill it, sooner or later, we are going to think that we know more than He does. He has to get us to the place where we are no longer running the show, but rather deferring to His wisdom.

And Moses took his wife and his sons, and set them upon an ass, and he returned to the land of Egypt: and Moses took the rod of God in his hand.

Exodus 4:20

When Moses approached the burning bush, God asked him what he held in his hand. Moses answered that he was holding a stick. It was a plain old stick that Moses threw down before God but when God gave it back to him, the Bible calls it "the rod of

God." It wasn't Moses' stick anymore. It was God's stick. This is what God is asking of every believer. If you want to follow God's will, you will go through a process like this, where God is going to ask "Will you really trust Me?" He is going to ask you to sacrifice something. He will ask you to lay down your life and turn it over to Him. If you keep control of your own life, it will never have any more power than what you can put behind it. By becoming a living sacrifice and turning your life over to God, you will gain God's strength.

Moses received much more in return than he gave. He gave up a stick, a dead piece of wood, and God gave him back something that turned a river into blood, parted a sea, caused hail to fall out of a clear sky, and water to gush from a rock. Moses received the power of God! You will always come out on top when you make a trade with God. God may ask for everything you have but He will give you everything He has in return. You will always be better off when you lay your life down for God.

One of the things that really helped me when I started following the Lord was ministering in nursing homes. I ministered two or three times a week. This was really good for me because I encountered people who were once very wealthy or successful in life, but the benefit of those things eluded them in old age. I don't believe we have to be decrepit and sick when we grow old, but old age is going to catch up with us. We are going to pass our prime someday.

Unless Jesus comes, every one of us is going to come to the end of our physical strength. The truth is that it doesn't take near that long before most of us crash and burn. We just need to recognize that we cannot accomplish God's will in our own strength and power. So when God asks us to make a total surrender and yield to Him, whatever He wants us to do, we just need to do it. Then we'll get His strength and power and be much better off.

Christ in You

Is not this the word that we did tell thee in Egypt, saying, Let us alone, that we may serve the Egyptians? For it had been better for us to serve the Egyptians, than that we should die in the wilderness. And Moses said unto the people, Fear ye not, stand still, and see the salvation of the LORD, which he will shew to you today: for the Egyptians whom ye have seen today, ye shall see them again no more forever. The LORD shall fight for you, and ye shall hold your peace.

Exodus 14:12-14

The Israelites had just left Egypt. They were camped in a valley with mountains on both sides of them, the Red Sea in front of them, and Pharaoh's army coming up behind them. It looked like they were trapped with nowhere to go, yet God instructed Moses to camp there. God hardened Pharaoh's heart to believe that the Israelites were entangled in the land. Pharaoh saw the situation as an opportunity to get revenge against Israel for the plagues and humiliation that God had enacted upon Egypt. Basically, the Lord set a trap for Pharaoh. God told Moses what was going to happen, but the people were in full scale revolt. In a panic, they said, "Why did you bring us out here to die? We should have stayed in Egypt." The situation didn't look promising from a logical standpoint.

The anointing of God came through Moses and he quieted them by saying, "Stand still and see the salvation of the Lord." He told them they wouldn't have to fight—God was going to fight for them. All of a sudden the revolt stopped. They were completely silent. Moses had stopped the uprising. But the Egyptians were still coming.

> *And the LORD said unto Moses, Wherefore criest thou unto me? speak unto the children of Israel, that they go forward: But lift thou up thy rod, and stretch out thine hand over the sea, and divide it: and the children of Israel shall go on dry ground through the midst of the sea.*
>
> *Exodus 14:15-16*

Somewhere in between Moses' bold statement to the Israelites and what the Lord said here, Moses apparently began to cry out, "God, what are we going to do?" He was asking God to do a miracle—to do something to stop the Egyptians. This seemed reasonable given the situation, but God said, "Why are you crying unto me? Take the rod, hold it out over the sea and part the sea." Basically the Lord was saying, "Don't you remember that you turned your life over to Me when you picked up the serpent by the tail? That's not your stick you're holding, it's My *rod*. Now take the authority I have given you and use it." This is a word for us today:

our life is not our own, Christ lives through us and we need to use the power He has given us to improve our situation (Galatians 2:20).

Instead of praying for God to do something when we get into a crisis situation, we need to recognize that we have the power of God living on the inside of us. Once we have turned our lives over to God, we have power over our circumstances. Cancer, illness, and every kind of lack should tremble in our presence. We need to quit begging God to do something, as if He hasn't done anything. God gave us power. We turned our lives over to Him, so now we need to take the power He gave us and command our situation to change. We need to use our God-given authority to do something about our problem.

God told Moses, *"Get up off your face, take the rod, and do something."* I am convinced that if Moses had stayed there begging and pleading with God, they would all have been destroyed. Prayer has its place, but there comes a time when you have to get up off your knees and do something—a time to believe God's Word and accept that He has given you power and authority to change your circumstances. Use your authority: command sickness to flee and order the devil to get out of your life. You can't ask God to rebuke the devil for you. He told *us* to resist the devil to make him flee (James 4:7). We have to be bold.

Trusting God in all circumstances comes from having a deep relationship with Him. You won't fully trust God until you have made yourself a living sacrifice and have seen Him come through for you. Believers should recognize that it is no longer they who live, but Christ living in them (Galatians 2:20). You won't have the boldness to fight against the wiles of the enemy unless you know that Christ lives in you. Once you have turned your life over to the Lord, you need to use the authority He has given you so you won't be overcome when the enemy comes against you in the wilderness.

It's true that you can't accomplish God's will in your own strength, but you have to balance that with the fact that you can do all things through Christ who strengthens you (Philippians 4:13). You need both sides of the equation in balance. *Without Christ I can do nothing, but Praise God, I'm not without Christ!* God will never leave us nor forsake us (Hebrews 13:5). Place no confidence in yourself; have great confidence in Christ, who lives in you. Confidence in God and humility are not opposing truths, they are two sides of the same coin. We need both perspectives to enjoy a healthy relationship with God and walk in victory.

Moses Strikes the Rock

The children of Israel spent 40 years in the wilderness. During that time there was an instance when God had Moses strike a rock with his rod and enough water flowed out of the rock to satisfy three million Jews—plus all of their animals (Exodus 17:6). It was absolutely miraculous. Toward the end of the 40 years, the people were without water again, but this time the Lord told Moses to speak to the rock instead of striking it (Numbers 20:8). Moses went before the people, stood before the rock, and began to rebuke the people for complaining. Then Moses took his rod and struck the rock, but nothing happened—because God told him to speak the rock, not hit it. Moses struck the rock a second time and water gushed out. But the Lord told Moses that he would not live to enter into the Promised Land because of his disobedience in striking the rock (Numbers 20:10-12).

By that time, Moses had spent one hundred and twenty years following God. All Moses did was hit the rock, yet God refused to allow him to enter into the Promised Land. I always heard this scripture explained saying that the rock symbolized Christ (1 Corinthians 10:4) so when Moses hit the rock a second time it was like trying to crucify Christ twice. In essence, Moses broke the symbolism God was trying to establish by showing that Christ, once crucified, cannot be crucified again (Hebrews 6:6). I can see the logic behind this teaching, but it seems harsh to me that God would make Moses miss his entire life's goal just because he broke a symbolic meaning.

I believe the real issue here was Moses' self-will. He had taken things into his own hands once before, when he killed the Egyptian, and it cost the children of Israel 30 years of extra bondage. After 40 years of leading the people through the wilderness, his self-will was beginning to rise up again. God told him to speak to the rock, but Moses thought it would be more dramatic to hit it. He was exerting his own wisdom and trying to do things his own way again. If God had failed to deal with Moses' self-will, the entire nation of Israel could have spent another 40 years in the wilderness. It wasn't just symbolism. God did this to protect Israel from Moses.

We don't ever learn the lesson of humility completely. It's not like we have one encounter with the Lord and then never have to deal with leaning on our own understanding or ability again. Moses laid his life down at the burning bush, but here he was veering back toward self-reliance. God had to bring Moses back to dependence on Him.

Some people think everything in the life of a Christian is supposed to work perfectly after you believe, but it doesn't happen that way. *God uses us in spite of who we are, not because of who we are.* Don't be upset if you believe for perfect health and then get a cold that ruins your record. You will still get over it in two days instead of two weeks. It's no big deal. It doesn't mean that God failed you. It just means that you are growing. You will never do anything perfectly. Perfectionism immobilizes people with anxiety because they are constantly worried about something going wrong. It makes people so cautious that they never get anything accomplished. People who change the world are people who aren't afraid to step out and take action.

We can learn a few lessons at Moses' expense. Instead of spending 40 years in the desert with scorpions and snakes, we can take these teachings to heart and make a decision that will change our lives. We don't have to be rung out in order for God to use us. If that's your experience, praise God, whatever it takes—but it doesn't have to be that way. The Holy Spirit can teach us by revelation that God's ways are better than our own plans. Lay your life down before God; give Him control. God will take your offering and give you back His life and power in return.

Chapter 9

Let Peace Rule

And let the peace of God rule in your hearts, to the which also ye are called in one body; and be ye thankful.

Colossians 3:15

The Greek word for *rule* comes from the root word from which we get our English word *umpire*, which means "to govern or arbitrate." We can understand this in the same way we understand the function of an umpire in baseball: once the umpire makes the call, it is decided. The pitcher hurls the ball toward home plate and the umpire calls it either a ball or a strike. His decision is final; there's no debate, no chance for a redo. The peace of God should act just like an umpire in our hearts—deciding which opportunities we should act on and which ones we should let pass by.

Peace is a fruit of the Holy Spirit, so you always have peace in your born-again spirit (Galatians 5:22-23). You may not always feel peace because you aren't always living out of your spirit. We can get caught up in our emotions or our thinking, but peace is always present within us. All we have to do is shut off the things that dominate us from the outside and follow the peace that is in our spirit.

The Holy Spirit is constantly bearing witness in our heart, but not always with words. Sometimes we just feel peace, or a lack of it, about doing something. We shouldn't do anything unless we have peace in our heart about doing it. This principle is the flip side of delighting yourself in the Lord (Psalm 37:4).

Many years ago, I planned a trip to Costa Rica. I had ministered there before and had a tremendous response, so they invited me back. I purchased my plane tickets early and was looking forward to preaching there again. A few weeks before the trip, I helped my mother move. While driving the moving truck from Texas to Colorado, I began to pray about my ministry opportunity in Costa Rica. As I prayed about the trip, I lost all desire to go. On the previous trip, we saw some terrific things happen and had a great time, so there wasn't any reason for me not to want to go back. I just lost my desire to go.

I knew that I needed to make sure I was hearing from God and not merely feeling an emotional reaction, so during the 17 hour drive to Colorado I worshipped God and prayed in tongues. The more I focused on God, the less I wanted to go to Costa Rica. I decided to let the peace of God rule in my heart. I couldn't come up with any particular reason, but I had zero peace about going. So I canceled my meeting and the people hosting the meeting got really upset. They had already done a lot of advertising and wanted to know why I was cancelling. I told them I didn't have a reason, I just didn't want to go. Of course, that wasn't a very spiritual answer so they were offended. I didn't know what to say to them except that I had lost my peace about going.

Three weeks later, I was at home in Colorado when I heard about a flight out of Mexico City that crashed during take-off. Everyone onboard the plane died. I think that's why the Lord took away my peace for that trip. If I had gone ahead with the meeting simply because I didn't have a logical reason to call it off, I probably would have died in that plane crash. But instead, I let the peace of God act as umpire—and it saved my life!

Before this happened, I learned the hard way to trust the leading of God's peace in my heart. While pastoring a church in Pritchett, Colorado, we saw a man raised from the dead, witnessed great things, and were making a difference in the community. Our church grew to 100 members in a town of only 144 people!

The few people who were in leadership in the church before I came were custom combiners. They were gone for six months out of the year harvesting crops. They wanted to put a new elder in place to help me run the church while they were gone, so they suggested a man who had been the only person to embrace me when I first arrived in town. He was a neat guy who was excited about what we were teaching. I didn't have any reason not to want him as an elder, except I didn't feel peace about it in my heart.

I told the other leaders that I didn't feel good about having him as an elder. They said, "Why not? Tell us what's wrong with him." But I didn't have an answer. I didn't know of anything that was wrong with him. They countered by telling me all of the reasons he looked like a good choice, yet all I had to say was, "I don't feel good about it." We talked for a long time and they basically shamed me until I gave in. By the end of the meeting, it was agreed that he would become the new elder.

Within a week after the combiners left town to go harvest wheat, the new elder turned into the devil personified. He started rumors that I was drinking, committing adultery, doing drugs, and stealing money from the church. Even though I didn't even take a salary from the church, he accused me of anything and everything you could think of. I had nothing but problems from him. It was terrible.

When all of this happened, I thought, "*I knew in my heart that we shouldn't have made him an elder!*" I didn't feel peace about it and went with logic instead of what I felt in my heart. I decided right then that I would never make the same mistake again. Since then, to the best of my ability, I have always let the peace of God rule in my heart.

A year or two after this incident, I felt a lack of peace about going to Costa Rica. Since I had learned my lesson about the elder and not following my peace, I wasn't about to ignore the lack of peace I was feeling in this situation—and it probably saved my life!

I think nearly everyone has encountered a similar experience some time in their life. At some time or another, we have all been at a major crossroad and made a logical decision that went against what we felt led to do in our heart. We wanted to go one way, but all logic and counsel suggested that we go in another—so we went with the logical decision. As soon as everything fell apart, we said, "I knew I wasn't supposed to do that." For no particular reason, we *knew* that we weren't supposed to do it, but we did it anyway because it looked like the right thing to do. When we listen, we will hear God speaking to us and leading us in the right direction.

Big and Little

Letting the peace of God rule in our heart is one of the best ways to discern His leadership. He will put a desire in our heart then it's up to us to evaluate whether or not we feel peace about doing it—as we confirm that it's from God. We need to spend extra time seeking the Lord to see if the idea still excites and blesses us. This not only applies to big decisions, like our life-long vocation; it applies to life's little details as well. Does God want you to hire a particular employee or buy a certain house? It's pretty simple. I pray about things and whatever I have the most peace about doing, that is what I go with.

We bought the building that our ministry is currently in for 3.25 million dollars, which was a huge step for us. We had to take out a loan to get the building; it was just an empty warehouse that needed another 3.2 million dollars worth of renovations. After we purchased the building, we spent nine months trying to obtain a construction loan for the renovations. Initially, the lender guaranteed us the construction loan. They said, "We wouldn't give you a loan for the building if we weren't planning to give you the construction loan." For nine months, the banker kept telling us that we would get the loan "next week." It was a difficult situation and we needed to do something, but they wouldn't give us the money. Finally, the banker said, "Why don't we just start the whole process over? We'll get a new appraisal and start the whole process over."

All I could see was another nine months of delays. Something didn't seem right, so I started praying. As I was praying that afternoon, I remembered some things that the Lord had spoken to me two years earlier. Someone had given me a prophecy that I wouldn't need to take out a loan, because I already had my *own* bank. When the Holy Spirit brought that to my remembrance, I thought, *I have my own bank? Where is it?* Then I recalled the rest of the prophecy: my ministry partners would be my financing. Somehow or another I hadn't associated the prophecy with the building program. As I was praying, the Lord brought the prophecy back to me and said, "I don't want you to take out a loan. I'm going to pay for this."

I don't know if you can relate to coming up with 3.2 million dollars, but at the rate our ministry was saving, it would have taken us more than a hundred years to come up with that kind of money! Obviously, that wasn't going to work. I knew that a commitment to renovate the building without taking out a loan would kill the ministry unless God came through in a big way. But I felt that God was leading me to trust Him for the money, so I wouldn't go back on the decision once it was made. Scripture says that a godly man will swear to his own hurt and change not (Psalm 15:4), so I told people that if I was going to do it debt free then I would do it debt free even if it took me a hundred years!

It was a big decision. Once I had the desire in my heart to build debt-free, I prayed about it for a week or two and then let the peace of God rule in my heart. The decision was potentially disastrous for the future of our ministry. We didn't have any evidence to suggest that we could raise 3.2 million dollars, but I had peace about it—so we decided to start the renovations without taking out a loan. Fourteen months later, we had 3.2 million dollars, the building was finished, and we moved in without the debt of a construction loan. It was one of the best decisions I have ever made. Even though it was illogical, we did it because I had peace in my heart about it. God's supernatural provision came through for us.

Peace, Be Still

Be still, and know that I am God.

Psalm 46:10

I believe we have made the Christian life harder than it needs to be. It's not difficult to have God lead us. We just love God with our whole heart and commit our lives unto Him, then as we delight in the Lord, He puts His desires in our hearts. When we come to a fork in the road, we just need to go in the direction we have the most peace about. But we can't live this way if we are constantly flooding our minds with the noise and junk of this world. Most Christians do not seek God or spend enough time in His presence to really feel what is in their hearts. They are led by external things, being pushed along in life by the crowd. Sometimes we have to be still in order to hear our heart.

Once I had a dream in which I saw a big banner with "Psalm 46:10" written on it. I have quoted this verse a thousand times, but at that moment I couldn't remember that verse to save my life. So I got out of bed, opened up my Bible, and found the scripture. It was such a vivid dream that I sat there thinking about that verse. I didn't know exactly what "being still" meant, but I decided that I was going to try being physically still, just to see if that was part of it.

Later that day, Jamie went shopping, so I was at the house alone for a while. I went outside, sat down in a chair, and for an hour and a half I never moved anything but my eyes. I sat as still as I possibly could. I wanted to see what would happen if I was really still. It took me a while to get totally still, but after I did, I started noticing things that I normally wouldn't have noticed.

We live in the Colorado mountains—where there's a lot of wildlife. I saw thousands of ants that I have never noticed before. A deer walked so close to me that I could almost touch it. I became so still that even a chipmunk came and sat on my foot. Sounds, like the wind blowing through the trees, that I never really paid any attention to, became loud. I became aware of all of these things that I typically never noticed before because I was always too busy going somewhere or doing something.

This principle can be applied to us spiritually as well. Sometimes we have to be still—no television or radio noise in the background. Instead of always talking when we pray, sometimes we need to be still and listen. I have a friend who spouts words like a machine gun when he prays. Once he gets going, he doesn't stop—*then he wonders why God never speaks to him.* God can't get a word in edgewise. We need to pretend like we are praying over a two-way radio every once in a while, and say "over," to give God a chance to speak. When we are still, the things that are in our heart come out and we begin to hear God speak to us.

This is one reason people who aren't seeking the Lord hate to be still. When we are still, a little homing device that God has planted in all of us starts going off. It makes us think about our lives and question whether or not we are experiencing all there is. People who are not seeking God don't want to be confronted by Him, so they drown Him out. They always have the TV or music on—they are always doing something. They can't be still because their thoughts will lead them to God, and they don't want to go there.

Life can get to be a treadmill that keeps you from resting because you are too busy just trying to keep up the pace. When you are on the treadmill, you don't have time to ask yourself, "Is this the life I want? Is this what God wants for me?" Many people go years without sitting down to take an inventory of their lives.

Everyone needs to look at their life now and again to inspect their options. See what your desires are and seek God to find out what you have peace about doing. Ask yourself where you want to be in five, ten, or twenty years. Are you doing what you want to be doing? Is your life headed in the direction you want it to be going? If you don't have peace about where you are right now or where you are going, you need to start making some changes.

If you aren't absolutely sure what changes to make, just start testing the waters. A boat has to be moving for the rudder to steer it. The rudder won't do anything when the boat is sitting still. In the same way, you have to be moving before God can give you direction. If you aren't sure what God wants you to do, let the peace of God rule in your heart and start taking small steps in the direction you have peace about. As you begin to step out, God can guide you. All of a sudden, things will begin to fall in line and you will see God moving in your life, which will encourage you to go a little further.

When I first started seeking God, I did all kinds of things. You might have to try a number of avenues before you find the right one. You might start off in one direction, only to see everything go wrong and lose all of your peace. Sometimes the way you discern God's will is by finding out what He *doesn't* want you to do—like when God gives you a *holy dissatisfaction.* If you don't have peace about what you are doing then don't go that direction.

I know this isn't deep—it's practical, and it can change your life. Anybody can do what I'm talking about. Every time you face a decision, God is speaking to you and giving you direction. He may not speak in an audible voice but He will guide you. Often, God will guide you by the peace in your heart. I believe that most people who seek God's will for their lives would discover significant direction simply by being still and allowing God's peace to rule in their hearts. Jesus is the Prince of Peace and He will show you the way you need to go.

Chapter 10

The Holy Spirit

But as it is written, Eye hath not seen, nor ear heard, neither have entered into the heart of man, the things which God hath prepared for them that love him.

1 Corinthians 2:9

The Apostle Paul was in the middle of defending his authority to the Corinthians when he wrote this scripture. He was quoting an Old Testament verse, but a large portion of the church has used this scripture to embrace the idea that we can never understand God or expect victory in this life. God's ways *are* higher than our ways (Isaiah 55:8)—but that doesn't mean He can't reveal Himself to us or lead us into victory. Paul was merely saying that in our natural physical ability, apart from the inspiration and the revelation of the Holy Spirit, we can't understand God. People stop at this verse and say, "See, we can't know God." But you can't stop there. You have to keep reading:

But God hath revealed them unto us by his Spirit: for the Spirit searcheth all things, yea, the deep things of God. For what man knoweth the things of a man, save the spirit of man which is in him? even so the things of God knoweth no man, but the Spirit of God. Now we have received, not the spirit of the world, but the spirit which is of God; that we might know the things that are freely given to us of God.

1 Corinthians 2:10-12

Paul isn't saying we can't *know*. He is saying that in ourselves, without the inspiration of God, we can't know His will. In our natural minds we don't know everything, but we have a mind in our spirits. These scriptures say that our born-again spirit has been infused with the knowledge of God, so we *can* understand the things of God.

Our spirit knows everything we need to know. We already have wisdom in our spirit. God understands that we live in a physical world and the Scripture says that if any man lacks wisdom let him ask God. The wisdom we receive doesn't come from heaven. God has already abounded toward us in all wisdom and prudence (Ephesians 1:8). The Bible says that we have a special anointing, or power, from God and our spirit knows all things (1 John 2:20). *Our job is to draw out what God has already put in us.*

Unless we know how to draw out the wisdom and power of God from our spirit, we will end up trying to discern God's will by judging our circumstances. King David wrote that no one should be like a horse or mule, which has no understanding and must be led around by bit and bridle (Psalm 32:8-9). We are supposed to be led by God, not our circumstances. Isaiah prophesied that we would hear a voice behind us saying, "This is the way, walk thou in it" (Isaiah 30:21). We should be led by the still small voice of God (1 Kings 19:12-13). Allowing our circumstances to dictate our course of action is no different than a mule being pulled this way and that way by a bit.

One night, the Apostle Paul had a dream of a man from Macedonia calling him over to help them (Acts 16:9). When he woke up in the morning, he knew that dream meant that God was sending him to minister to the people of Macedonia. So Paul and Silas traveled to Macedonia and entered the city of Philippi. Within days they were arrested, beaten, and locked in the lowest part of the dungeon (Acts 16:23-24).

In similar circumstances, I think most of us would say, "Well, this must not have been God." We would reason that God would never lead us to do something that would land us in jail. But circumstances are not a reliable indicator of God's will. Paul *was* following God's leading and going to Philippi was exactly what God told him to do. Observing circumstances is not an accurate way to discern God's will.

The spirit on the inside of us knows all things (1 John 2:20 with Colossians 3:10 and 1 Corinthians 2:16). Part of following God's will involves learning to listen to the voice of God inside of us and obeying it no matter what. In our spirit, we have supernatural God-ordained wisdom; by tapping into it, we will begin to see things that are hidden to our natural mind.

Drawing it Out

Howbeit we speak wisdom among them that are perfect: yet not the wisdom of this world, nor of the princes of this world, that come to nought: But we speak the wisdom of God in a mystery, even the hidden wisdom, which God ordained before the world unto our glory.

1 Corinthians 2:6-7

God's wisdom trumps natural wisdom. Paul said, "We speak the wisdom of God in a mystery, even the hidden wisdom." This wisdom that is hidden from the natural mind, but it isn't hidden *from* you—it is hidden *for* you.

One of the first things I did when the news media announced that the economy was in recession was to start boldly proclaiming that God supplies all of my needs according to His riches in glory by Christ Jesus (Philippians 4:19). I'm not limited to this world's economy and God has proved it. In the first six months after the recession hit in October 2008, the stock that Jamie and I owned made a 61% profit—while the stock market itself went down 51%. You can do the same thing if you believe that God is your source, instead of this natural world.

Every month since October 2008, our ministry's income has exceeded income for that same month in previous years. I think our increase was something like 28% this last year—during a "recession." The wisdom of the world would tell you that it's not possible to prosper during an economic downturn in the way we have, but our prosperity isn't coming by using the wisdom of this world.

This is another example of why renewing our mind with the Word of God is essential. God's Word reveals His will and knowing His will gives us the faith to believe for the impossible— and see it come to pass. Knowledge of God's Word is power. It's how we know what God has promised us and what we can have faith to believe He will supply. But aside from reading the Word, the Apostle Paul reveals another way for us to tap into the wisdom in our spirit:

> *Follow after charity, and desire spiritual gifts, but rather that ye may prophesy. For he that speaketh in an unknown tongue speaketh not unto men, but unto God: for no man understandeth him; howbeit in the spirit he speaketh mysteries.*
>
> *1 Corinthians 14:1-2*

This scripture is part of the same letter in which the Apostle Paul said, "We speak the wisdom of God in a mystery." (1 Cor. 2:6-7) In this verse, he says that when you are speaking in tongues, you are speaking mysteries. Paul was a man who helped change the world. It was said of him that he was among those "who turned the world upside down" (Acts 17:6). He wrote almost half of the New Testament. Do you know where he received all that wisdom?

When he was born again, God put His supernatural wisdom in Paul's born-again spirit. Just as any other believer, Paul had an unction from the Holy One and he knew all things (1 John 2:20)— he had the mind of Christ (1 Corinthians 2:16). Paul says that he drew the knowledge out of his spirit by speaking in tongues. Even though our spirit knows all things, we still have to get the knowledge into our natural understanding. Paul said,

> *For if I pray in an unknown tongue, my spirit prayeth, but my*
> *understanding is unfruitful.*
>
> 1 Corinthians 14:14

When we speak in tongues, our spirit prays—the part of us that knows all things (1 John 2:20), —is renewed in knowledge (Colossians 3:10), and has the mind of Christ (1 Corithians 2:16). This is the same part of us that always has peace and love; it doesn't have any questions or problems. Our spirit prays the hidden wisdom of God in a mystery, under the inspiration of the Holy Spirit.

One of the most important things we can do when we come up against a difficult situation is pray in tongues. Our born-again spirit, which has the mind of Christ and knows all things, prays our answer when we speak in tongues. Our spirit prays the wisdom we need and gives us instruction. Scripture says that when we speak in tongues, our understanding is unfruitful. In other words, our mind doesn't understand what we are saying. But Paul tells us how to unravel the mystery,

> *Wherefore let him that speaketh in an unknown tongue pray*
> *that he may interpret.*
>
> 1 Corinthians 14:13

We are speaking the hidden wisdom of God when we pray in tongues. It isn't gibberish; it's just that our mind doesn't understand spiritual things. As we pray, the wisdom of God comes right out of our mouth. It comes out in a language we don't understand; we just need to get an interpretation. Speaking in tongues is like flipping a supernatural switch—we turn on a powerful generator and the life and wisdom of God that is in our spirit starts coming out of our mouth. All we have to do is ask God to give us an interpretation of what we are praying from our spirit and He will reveal to us the wisdom we are speaking in tongues.

Paul gave instruction that if anyone speaks in tongues in a church service, it must be interpreted in a language the people understand so all of the listeners will be edified (1 Corithians 14:27-28). But speaking in tongues isn't just for church services. Paul said, "I thank my God, I speak with tongues more than ye all: Yet in the church I had rather speak five words with my understanding, that by my voice I might teach others also, than ten thousand words in an unknown tongue" (1 Corithians 14:18-19). He spoke in tongues more than the entire church of Corinth put together. He didn't do most of this during church; he spoke in tongues privately.

Speaking in tongues isn't just for the purpose of prophesy or ministering to other people. The gift of tongues that operates in a church service is a ministry of the Holy Spirit, given to edify and build up the church body—not everybody has that gift. That gift of tongues is what Scripture is talking about when it says, "Do all speak with tongues?" The obvious answer is "no" (1 Corinthians

12:30), but that statement is a reference to the *gift* of speaking in tongues and interpretation that functions within a church service. Not everybody has a *ministry* of speaking in tongues, but every born-again believer who is filled with the Holy Spirit has *the ability* to speak in tongues. Jesus said, "and these signs shall follow them that believe; in my name shall they cast out devils; they shall speak with new tongues" (Mark 16:17).

Edify Yourself

Speaking in tongues is not something you do one time in church, in order to prove that you are filled with the Holy Spirit. It is something you should be doing on a regular basis. It's your spirit man praying. Your spirit is where your new life is—it's where the power of God is. Your natural mind doesn't understand what your spirit is praying, but that is to be expected.

> *But the natural man receiveth not the things of the Spirit of God: for they are foolishness unto him: neither can he know them, because they are spiritually discerned.*
>
> *1 Corinthians 2:14*

Spiritual things are foolishness to the natural mind. If you speak in tongues for more than five minutes, your mind is going to say, "This is silly, what am I doing?" The carnal part of you will rise up and try to get you back into the natural realm, where it feels comfortable. You have to make a decision to continue speaking in tongues in spite of what your mind is thinking. You edify yourself when you speak in tongues (1 Corithians 14:4), and promote spiritual growth. Speaking in tongues is an act of faith; it requires you to cross the barrier between carnal thinking and being focused on God.

It is impossible for you to pray in tongues over a long period of time and keep your mind focused on carnal ungodly things. A mind that is focused on carnal things is not attentive to spiritual things, because the carnal mind is hostile to God. So a mind focused on the information coming in through your five senses will always be opposed to God. On the other hand, if you persist in speaking in tongues, your attention will shift to spiritual things—which brings life and peace (Romans 8:6-7).

You can do something with your mind as you pray in tongues and still have perfect comprehension, because your spirit is praying—not your brain. You can read the Bible while you are speaking in tongues and understand what you are reading perfectly. You can't do that quoting "Mary Had a Little Lamb", because you are quoting out of your mind and trying to read with your mind at the same time. But when you are praying in tongues, your spirit is praying—not your brain. This is one of the things that reveals that speaking in tongues is supernatural. You aren't just making up words. The sounds don't come from your brain; they come out of your spirit.

When I first started speaking in tongues, I used to do it for one to five hours a day. I discovered that while the spirit is praying, the brain is unoccupied. You can't turn your brain off so it's going to think about something. The mind will wander while you are praying in tongues and start thinking of all sorts of things. The way I dealt with this was to pray with my mind as I prayed with my spirit. This helped me focus my thoughts on God.

As I prayed, things would suddenly come to me. I would think of people I hadn't thought of in years. All of a sudden they would come to mind so I would pray for them with my mind; at the same time I was praying in tongues out of my mouth. At first, I didn't connect the two, but when I was done praying I would call the person who came to my mind and talk to them. Each time, my call was an answer to prayer and they would say, "You must have been hearing from God to call me right now."

One time, God put a friend of mine on my heart as I was praying in tongues so I felt like calling him. His wife answered the phone when I called, and as soon as she heard my voice she hung up. I thought to myself, *"Boy, that went really well."* As I was sitting there trying to figure out what I might have done wrong, she called back a moment later and explained what was going on. Her husband had just been forced out of the ministry because of some bad decisions. They lost their home and she was living with her mother at nearly 60 years old. Their entire life had come undone.

She said, "We've traveled the world helping other people and I was just sitting here praying, and said, 'God, why don't You have somebody minster to us? I know that we are living with my mother and our phone number has changed, but You're God, You could at least have somebody call. If You really love us, why don't you have somebody call?'"

The phone rang right when she finished praying. She picked it up and heard me say, "This is Andrew Wommack." She was so shocked that she hung up. But then she called back and I was able to minister to her. *When you pray in tongues God will speak to you and reveal things that you can't know with your physical mind.*

On another occasion, Jamie and I felt led to stop in a little town of 100 people while we were driving through the middle of nowhere in Colorado. We stopped to see some old friends we hadn't spoken to for over a decade. They thought we were a little too radical and had tried to turn us away from the ministry, creating a rift between us. The town was small so it was pretty easy to find out where the Baptist pastor lived.

We knocked on the front door and my old friend Joseph opened it. The moment he saw me, all of the blood drained out of his face. He stood there looking at me and didn't say a word. So I asked if we could come inside and he silently turned aside to let us walk in. We walked in and his wife was kneeling down praying at the coffee table. She looked up and turned white also.

We all sat down, but they just stared at us white-faced and silent. Finally, I asked, "Is everything okay?" Joseph told me that they had resigned their position at the church and their life was in turmoil. He said they had just been kneeling around the coffee table asking God to send someone to help them. They said, "We'll take anybody Lord...*anybody*." Our knock at the door came while they were still praying. We were the last people they would normally have let in, but God put us together supernaturally and we became great friends again. God also restored them and put them back in the ministry. It was awesome!

Things like this happen when you pray in tongues. As you pray, God will speak things to you. Interpretation doesn't mean that you pray in tongues one moment and then ask for an interpretation in English right after. As you pray in tongues, your understanding will become fruitful. You will get a mental understanding of the things your spirit is praying; it's the hidden wisdom of God being drawn out into your natural awareness.

For about the first two years that I spoke in tongues, I had doubts that it was really God. I was raised a Baptist and had been told that the devil will give you a "demon tongue." I still had those thoughts come to me after being baptized in the Holy Spirit. Even though I knew speaking in tongues was from God, I wasn't totally confident.

One morning I prayed in tongues for two hours and fought thoughts of unbelief the whole time. I was thinking, *Is this really God? Is this really the Holy Spirit? Or am I just making this stuff up?* As I was praying, a man I hadn't seen in four years knocked on my door. He was crying. He just walked in, sat down, and started telling me his problems. My first thought was that I had wasted the previous two hours praying in tongues, when I could have been doing something really spiritual that might have helped this guy. But then I realized I wouldn't even have known to pray for him.

I hadn't seen, or even thought of him, in four years. Suddenly it dawned on me that I had been praying in tongues for him for the previous two hours.

Immediately, I knew his problems. I stopped him in mid-sentence and said, "Let me tell you what's going on." I told him what was wrong and he was totally shocked. He knew it had to be God because there was no way I could have known what was happening. He knew God was speaking to him. As soon as he understood that God was supernaturally working in his situation, he was totally set free. It was a confirmation to him that I wasn't merely giving him advice, but that the Holy Spirit was interpreting the situation. I was able to minister to him from the power of God instead of from my own wisdom and understanding. Those two hours of speaking in tongues had paid off, even when I was struggling with doubt.

This is why getting a mental understanding of the things you are praying about in tongues is important. You don't need to stop and receive a word-for-word interpretation as you pray. You only have to be inspired in your thoughts. Whenever I don't know what to do, I pray in tongues and ask God for an interpretation. I say, "Father, give me wisdom. Show me what I need to know." I know wisdom resides in my spirit and I pray it out by speaking in tongues and receiving an interpretation. It results in supernatural revelation.

Some of you may think, "I wonder if these stories are really proof that speaking in tongues is from God? Maybe those were just coincidences." If I had the space, I could give you hundreds of examples that prove speaking in tongues is from God. You are too late to try to convince me that this doesn't work. I know it works. It has been working in my life for a long, *long* time.

Earlier I wrote about needing 3.2 million dollars to renovate our building in Colorado Springs. When the banker told me that we were going to have to start the loan process all over, I prayed. I was busy at the office so I didn't hear anything right then. Once I got home, I went for a walk on my property. As I walked, I prayed in tongues and asked for an interpretation. I wasn't even ten minutes down the trail before a prophecy came back to mind that I didn't need a bank—my partners would be my bank. I had thoughts come to me that hadn't crossed my mind in over a year, revelations that ultimately solved my problem. All of the renovation was completed without taking out a loan because I prayed in tongues and God gave me wisdom how to accomplish it.

Power for Living

When you have a need, don't ask God for help and then wait around to hear an audible voice echo down from the heavens. In your spirit, you have the mind of Christ. All you have to do is pray in tongues and ask for interpretation. Your spirit will intercede for you and pray exactly what you need to know. The answer may not come within the first five minutes. It may take a period of time. Like I said, it took me two years to get to where praying in tongues was deeply confirmed in me and I didn't have any more doubts.

It may take a period of time for you to get your mind renewed enough in faith that you can truly focus on God while speaking in tongues. Nonetheless, in your spirit you have the hidden wisdom of God and praying in tongues will draw it out.

I believe this is how the Apostle Paul received his revelation of God's grace. He wrote in his letter to the Galatians that when he was converted, he didn't go back to Jerusalem. He didn't receive his revelation from the disciples, or any other man; he received it directly from God (Galatians 1:11-12). Paul spent three and a half years praying in the desert to get his revelation (Galaltians 1:17-19). I believe he was praying in tongues and drawing that revelation out of his spirit.

The Jews of that time memorized the first five books of the Bible, so Paul already knew the Old Testament scriptures inside and out. He had knowledge of God's Word, but he needed to understand it so he prayed in tongues. He said the message he preached was the hidden wisdom of God in a mystery (1 Corithians 2:6-7); by praying in tongues, he was praying the hidden wisdom of God out of his spirit. As Paul prayed, God gave him a revelation of grace that is still transforming lives.

The Apostle Peter wrote in his letter that Paul's letters contained "things hard to be understood." The unlearned, or carnal people, wrestled with this along with the other scriptures (2 Peter 3:16). Peter confirmed that Paul's writings were Scripture and said they were hard to understand. Peter was a man who lived with

Jesus 24 hours a day for more than three years, yet he didn't understand the grace of God at the level that Paul did.

One time, Paul actually had to rebuke Peter openly for mistreating the Gentile believers (Galatians 2:11). Paul had a greater revelation of the grace of God and true nature of Jesus than people who lived with Him, because he received his revelation by the spirit, not by observation or intellect. It's possible that there was more involved in receiving his revelation than praying in tongues, we don't know, but I believe praying in tongues was a large part of it. Without a doubt, we can know things by the spirit better than we can by sight, feeling, or our carnal mind.

We aren't just natural beings; we are supernatural. When we get born again, we become a new creature (2 Corithians 5:17). We have power on the inside of us. We have the Spirit of God living on the inside of us (1 Corithians 6:19). Many Christians feel powerless to make changes in their lives, but that isn't true. We have God's power and authority that Jesus purchased for us on the cross. Once we know who we are and how to release the power of God within us, sickness and poverty don't stand a chance. I believe that praying in tongues is essential in releasing what's in our spirit. It will make our understanding fruitful and God will give us revelation.

Often when I pray in tongues, I don't get a specific revelation instantly. But later, for instance, when I go to a large meeting and am praying for people, the Lord will show me things and give me words of knowledge. He will show me things about people that I couldn't possibly know by my own natural understanding. Those words of knowledge enable me to call out specific healings the Lord is performing. This builds people's faith and miracles begin to happen. I'm not special; I just pray in tongues and God shows me what I need to know when the time comes.

Praying in Tongues Is for Today's Church

I pray in tongues all the time. Many people don't understand how important praying in tongues is. The devil has fought speaking in tongues because he knows how powerful it is. Religious people will sometimes say that speaking in tongues is "of the devil." But if speaking in tongues is of the devil, why can't you go into a bar and hear people speaking in tongues? Why don't criminals pray in tongues? It's an argument that doesn't even make sense. The Bible specifically says, "Forbid not to speak with tongues" (1 Corithians 14:39). It is a command from God, but many religious people say that speaking in tongues passed away with the apostles.

The Bible says that speaking in tongues will not pass away until that which is perfect has come (1 Corithians 13:10). Some try to argue that speaking in tongues has passed away because *"that which is perfect"* is the Bible. I agree that the Bible is perfect, but that is not what this scripture is talking about. The scripture says we will see the Lord "face-to-face" *and* knowledge will pass away at the same time as speaking in tongues passes away (1 Corithians 13:8-12). We haven't seen Jesus face-to-face and knowledge hasn't passed away.

"*That which is perfect*" refers to our glorified body. Therefore, the scripture is saying that speaking in tongues will pass away when Jesus comes. We won't need to speak in tongues in heaven because our carnal nature will be gone, allowing our spirit to dominate. But until that time, we need to continue to pray in tongues.

Speaking in tongues empowers us to discern and follow God's will. *We have everything we need to follow God's will in our spirit—* we just aren't using it. We love the light of our TV more than we love the light of God's Word. When we spend time praying in tongues, getting our minds focused on the Lord and asking Him for wisdom, He will lead and guide us. We need to ask the Lord to reveal what we are praying in tongues and we will see supernatural things start to happen.

Now, let me put one qualification on this. Don't pray in tongues and then assume that the first thought that comes to your mind is from God. It has to match up with the nature and the will of God as expressed through His Word. If your first thought after speaking in tongues is "I think I need a new spouse," then that's not from God. God's leading will never be contrary to His Word. When you first get started discerning God's leading, it's a good idea to have mature Christians in your life who can help you judge whether or not the desires you have are from God. As with all spiritual things, there is a maturation process involved in speaking in tongues.

I promise you that praying in tongues merely during the time you spend commuting to work in your car can transform you.

You could change your life by spending no more time praying in tongues than you already spend sitting in traffic. Pray in tongues instead of listening to junk on the radio about falling off of some bar stool, your dog leaving, losing your truck, or everything else. You are sitting in traffic anyway, so you don't have much else to do. Use that time to build yourself up and promote spiritual growth.

The Baptism of the Holy Spirit

> *But ye shall receive power, after that the Holy Ghost is come upon you: and ye shall be witnesses unto me both in Jerusalem, and in all Judaea, and in Samaria, and unto the uttermost part of the earth.*

> *Acts 1:8*

If you don't have this gift of speaking in tongues, you need it. God has placed Himself on the inside of every born-again believer, but there's more to the Christian life than the initial born-again experience. You need the baptism of the Holy Spirit to draw out the power God has placed inside of you and to pray in tongues. Speaking in tongues isn't something you do just to have a shiver run up and down your spine or to feel the presence of the Lord. It's much more powerful than that. You need the baptism of the Holy Spirit in order to be an effective witness and flow in the gifts of the Spirit.

Jesus told His disciples, "Behold, I send the promise of my Father upon you: but tarry ye in the city of Jerusalem, until ye be endued with power from on high" (Luke 24:49). Jesus didn't want the disciples out on their own trying to advance His kingdom. He wanted them to be filled with the power of the Holy Spirit. *In every example in the book of Acts where people received the Holy Spirit, it is either stated or implied in the text that they spoke in tongues.* Speaking in tongues is the initial outward sign of the baptism of the Holy Spirit.

You don't need to "tarry" until the Lord deems you worthy to be filled with the Holy Spirit. Some churches teach that you have to get every sin out of your life before God will baptize you in the Holy Spirit. They teach that you can't have any problems because God won't fill a dirty vessel. But God doesn't have any other kind of vessel to fill! If you could get holy without the Holy Spirit, you wouldn't need the Holy Spirit. The very fact that you have problems means that you are a candidate to receive the Holy Spirit. Don't let some failure make you think that God will not fill you with His Spirit.

> *What? know ye not that your body is the temple of the Holy Ghost which is in you, which ye have of God, and ye are not your own?*
>
> *1 Corinthians 6:19*

The Word of God says that you become the temple of the Living God when you are born again. God made you so He could fill you with His power. So there is no way He would refuse to give you the Holy Spirit. You were created to be God's temple. He wants to fill you with the Holy Spirit more than you want to be filled.

170

If a son shall ask bread of any of you that is a father, will he give him a stone? or if he ask a fish, will he for a fish give him a serpent? Or if he shall ask an egg, will he offer him a scorpion? If ye then, being evil, know how to give good gifts unto your children: how much more shall your heavenly Father give the Holy Spirit to them that ask him?

Luke 11:11-13

You don't need to beg and plead for God to baptize you with the Holy Spirit, you just have to be born again. Jesus is the one who baptizes you in the Holy Spirit, but the world cannot receive Him (John 14:16-17). No Jesus—no Holy Spirit. But if you are born again, God wants you to be filled with the power of the Holy Spirit with the evidence of speaking in tongues. God wants to give it and you need it. You might be thinking, "Do I have to speak in tongues?" No, you don't have to—you *get* to. It isn't a requirement for being saved; it's a benefit.

I guarantee you are going to need the baptism of the Holy Spirit to find, follow, and fulfill God's will for your life. You can't do it on your own. The Holy Spirit will guide you and show you things coming down the pike (John 16:13). The Holy Spirit is sent to reveal Jesus. He is our Teacher (John 14:26). You need His power in your life to accomplish God's plans for you.

One thing you need to understand about speaking in tongues is that the Holy Spirit inspires the words, but you have to speak them. The Holy Spirit isn't going to take control of your body and speak for you. God is a gentleman. He doesn't force Himself on anyone. He doesn't take control of people.

And they were all filled with the Holy Ghost, and began to speak with other tongues, as the Spirit gave them utterance.

Acts 2:4

The Spirit gave utterance, but the believers did the speaking. The Holy Spirit inspires you to speak, but you have to open up your mouth and utter the sounds. It is going to be your voice, affected by your accent. It's an act of faith: the Holy Spirit inspires by faith you do the speaking.

For example, when I minister I believe God is speaking through me, but He doesn't take my mouth and make me speak. If I prayed and asked God to speak through me and not let me say anything wrong, and then just opened my mouth and waited on Him to make the vocal chords move, nothing would happen. It doesn't happen that way. When I speak, words come out in my Texan accent with my sense of humor and personality. But I believe the words are inspired of God.

Likewise, when you speak in tongues, God doesn't force you to do it. You can't talk in tongues with your mouth closed. You have to open your mouth and begin to make sounds and believe, by faith, that God is inspiring it. Don't worry about what it sounds like. I've heard that some tribes only speak in clicks of the tongue and others in just different whistles, but they are known languages.

Sometimes speaking in tongues starts out the same way as when little children learn to talk. Their words may not sound like "Mommy" or "Daddy," but their parents know what they are trying to say. In the same way, our heavenly Father listens to our heart and loves that we are trying to communicate with Him from our spirit. As we keep praying in tongues, our prayer language will become more fluent over time—just like a child's does. Just start speaking. Don't quit.

God gives the Holy Spirit to everyone who asks of Him. If you recognize that you need the Holy Spirit and want to be filled with His presence, then say the prayer at the end of this chapter. It's the same prayer I have used to see thousands of people receive the baptism of the Holy Spirit.

Don't judge whether or not you receive the Holy Spirit by how you feel when you pray. Some people have great emotional experiences when they are filled with the Holy Spirit, while others don't. I didn't feel a thing—but I received the Holy Spirit. He lives on the inside of me. *God is going to give you the Holy Spirit when you ask,* so you only need to ask once—you don't need to beg. Trust that God has given you the Holy Spirit, whether you feel anything or not. Say this prayer one time and then begin to thank Him for filling you with the Holy Spirit.

Father, I thank You that I am the temple of the Holy Spirit. I now open up the doors of this temple. Holy Spirit, I welcome You to come and fill me and give me supernatural power. I welcome You to renew my mind, so that I can think supernaturally instead of naturally, and see Your power released into my life. And I ask for this gift of speaking in tongues. I pray this in Jesus' name. Amen.

Rejoice!

If you prayed that prayer and believed in your heart, you are now baptized in the Holy Spirit and you have the ability to speak in tongues! Open up your mouth and begin to utter the words that the Holy Spirit is inspiring you to speak. Don't let the fear of sounding silly stop you. The Apostle Paul said that the natural man doesn't understand the things of the spirit because they are foolishness to him (1 Corinthians 2:14). Your mind isn't going to understand the words that come from your lips, but that's okay. Speak out the words that you can feel rising up within you and don't try to interpret them with your natural mind. As you pray, focus your mind on the love God has for you and who the Word of God says you are.

Continue to pray in tongues by faith and ask God to give you the interpretation. This is going to start you down a road to seeing the supernatural power of God manifest in your life while giving you the ability to follow God's leading with more than just your natural mind.

Chapter 11

In It to Win It

I t's one thing to find God's will and start moving in the right direction, but it's another to stay with it over the long haul. Anybody can start, but it's the people who stick with it and finish that really make a difference. We have all seen people who rise to popularity and influence like a shooting star and then burn out just as quickly. A lot of people seem to burn out almost from the start. Unfortunately, the body of Christ is cluttered with people who have fallen by the wayside.

I was part of the Charismatic movement during the 1970s, when millions of people were touched by the power of God in a significant way. But not all of those people are still seeking God today. I've heard a statistic that said up to 70% of Charismatics no longer attend church. Our churches wouldn't have enough seats for everyone if they did!

The fact that you are reading a book about God's will is an indication that you are serious about your relationship with Him. You aren't just going to church on Sunday to pay a debt or do your duty. You are excited and seeking the things of God. I applaud you for your efforts; you are off to a great start. But not every person who gets off to a good start is going to finish his or her race. I'm not trying to be negative. I just want you to recognize the importance of learning how to fulfill God's will in your life, once you find it and begin to follow it.

Fortunately, I have some tips to help you stay on track. God doesn't determine that His power in your life will cease after a certain length of time and then you will have to get a fresh touch from Him again, as if His power comes with an expiration date. No, it's totally up to you whether or not you stay full of God and excited about His plans for your life. I think this is good news because it means that if you aren't keyed up about following God, you can do something to get excited about the things of God.

Obedience

My teaching focuses on the grace of God. I try to get people free from the misconception that they must earn God's love or from thinking that God will only move in their lives when they do everything right. God has never had anyone *qualified* working for him yet—none of us deserve His love. We just have to humble ourselves and receive His love as a gift. Our ministry's focus on God's grace is one reason, I believe, that God has raised us up. Grace just isn't being emphasized enough in the body of Christ. Many people don't understand the simple truth that God isn't mad at them.

The grace of God is the Gospel message but it sometimes causes a pendulum effect in people. In my estimation, the body of Christ is way out of balance on the side of legalism—trying to be holy and earn God's approval. Sometimes when people hear the good news of God's grace and realize salvation doesn't depend upon living a holy life, they swing clear over to the other extreme of thinking that it doesn't matter what they do.

I'm not necessarily talking about saying they revert to living in sin, but sometimes people who were caught up in legalism quit seeking the Lord with all of their heart because they think everything is up to God. They don't recognize the balance between grace and faith.[2] Obedience may be a dirty word to some, but we have to learn to obey God if we want to finish our race and cross the finish line as a winner. Obedience is essential to fulfilling God's will in our lives.

> *Come now, and let us reason together, saith the Lord: though your sins be as scarlet, they shall be as white as snow; though they be red like crimson, they shall be as wool. If ye be willing and obedient, ye shall eat the good of the land.*
>
> *Isaiah 1:18-19*

No one's sins have ever changed from crimson to being white as snow through their own goodness. This only happens by grace. We have a Savior who paid for our sin and that is the only way sin

---

[2] This is a topic that deserves more attention than I can give it here. I have written a book called *"Living in the Balance of Grace and Faith"* that goes into far more detail. Also, you can access a free audio teaching on the AWM website at: http://www.awmi.net/extra/audio/1064.

gets dealt with. This verse goes on to say that we have to be willing and obedient in order to eat the good of the land. God deals with us based on His grace, but we have to obey what He tells us to do if we are going to finish our race and accomplish His plans.

Don't get me wrong: disobeying God doesn't change His grace nature. God still loves us. He isn't going to be upset with us, He accepts us through Jesus. Many people preach that if you don't obey God, you won't prosper. This leaves the impression that God is going to snub us or put us on the shelf because we didn't do what He told us to. They also say, "God won't use a dirty vessel." I want you to know that God doesn't have any other kind of vessel to use! We can't do everything right. God's purpose for us is completely separate from what we deserve.

Won't vs. Can't

Obeying God in order to experience all of the blessings He desires to give us is not the same as saying that God won't use us *unless* we obey Him. It isn't that God won't, so much as He *can't*. If we don't follow God's leading, Satan is going to take advantage of our disobedience. Then the enemy will come into our life to steal, kill, and destroy.

> *Know ye not, that to whom ye yield yourselves servants to obey, his servants ye are to whom ye obey; whether of sin unto death, or of obedience unto righteousness?*
>
> *Romans 6:16*

Whoever we obey and make the master of our life is going to control us. God calls us, but in order to fulfill our purpose we have to follow His leading. If I was God, I wouldn't have picked me to do what I'm doing. It's not like I have everything going for me. God chose me *in spite of* who I am; that's grace. But if I hadn't obeyed Him and followed His leading, I wouldn't be where I am today. I wouldn't be seeing people's lives changed and our ministry wouldn't be successful. I had to take steps to obey the Lord. God's love for me remains the same whether I obey Him or not, but the potential for His love to work through me to transform others depends upon me yielding to His leadership.

I can't tell you how many people over the years have told me that they were sure God told them to do some particular thing, but they had a thousand reasons why they couldn't do it. They told me about their own natural limitations. They told me they didn't have enough money. They told me how this, that, and the other thing happened.

I actually had a lady tell me she knew God was calling her to go to Charis Bible College, but she said, "I have two dogs. What would I do? How could I come to Bible school if I have two dogs?" I told her, "Just shoot 'em." Of course, I didn't really want her to shoot her dogs. I was just trying to help her see what is truly important. It's amazing the little things we let stand in the way. We say, "Well, I have a goldfish and a hangnail. I couldn't possibly do what you are asking me to do Lord."

You are never going to fulfill God's calling on your life waiting around for every possible circumstance to line up perfectly. Jamie and I haven't done everything right the first time, but we have been quick to obey. We have stepped out when God called us to. We have done a few things in ways that I wouldn't necessarily recommend, and we have made some mistakes along the way, but we have always tried to obey God, even when it looked like following Him wasn't in our best interest. In order to fulfill our purpose, we have to be willing to obey God no matter what!

This is so simple, yet so many people who know what God is calling them to do won't step out because they are afraid of the cost. You can't fulfill God's will if you are afraid to step out and pursue it. Following God is going to cost you something. I can guarantee you that not everyone is going to support your decision. Proverbs says, "The fear of man bringeth a snare: but whoso putteth his trust in the LORD shall be safe" (Proverbs 29:25). If you need to have people's approval before you step out on what God calls you to do, you are never going to make it.

Doer of the Word

But be ye doers of the word, and not hearers only, deceiving your own selves. For if any be a hearer of the word, and not a doer, he is like unto a man beholding his natural face in a glass: For he beholdeth himself, and goeth his way, and straightway forgetteth what manner of man he was. But whoso looketh into the perfect law of liberty, and continueth therein, he being

not a forgetful hearer, but a doer of the work, this man shall be
blessed in his deed.

James 1:22-25

It isn't enough just to hear God's voice, you have to *do* what He says in order to fulfill your purpose in life. God isn't going to give you step number two or step number ten, if you haven't obeyed step number one. You move into God's will for your life by stages: the good, the acceptable, and the perfect (Romans 12:2). God's will is always perfect but the degree to which you experience His perfect will changes relative to how much you cooperate with His plans. God shows you things step by step, which means you have to act on what He leads you to do before you will ever see the next step.

Hearing and obeying God—or failing to obey—causes a ripple effect in your life. We know, for instance, that we should give money to support the preaching of the Gospel. The Bible teaches us to honor the Lord with our substance and with the first fruits of our increase (Proverbs 3:9). People know this but they don't obey. Then they wonder why other things in their lives aren't working. Jesus said if you aren't faithful in that which is least, you won't be faithful over much (Luke 16:10). In context, Jesus was saying that money is the least area you can trust God for. Trusting God with your finances is the smallest use of your faith. If you don't trust God with your money, you won't trust Him in other areas either.

A lot of people say they trust God for their salvation, but they grasp at their money like they don't trust Him to provide for their physical needs. How can you trust God with your eternal redemption, but not trust Him for "that which is least?" You can't do the greatest, if you can't do the least. You can't lift 200 pounds if you're not able to lift 20. Likewise, you can't do great things for God unless you can trust Him with your finances.

Every one of the mature Christians I know is a giver, without exception. They all trust God. You can't become a mature believer without trusting God in your finances. Conversely, I know a lot of Christians who look good on the outside, but I'm not sure if they are still going to be following God the next time I see them. Those are the people who don't trust God in their giving. Giving is an indicator of where you put your trust.

Trusting God in the area of your finances isn't just for "super-saints." Trusting God is basic to our faith. Some people know what the Word of God says about finances, but they aren't doing it. Then they wonder why they aren't prospering or being healed in their bodies. It isn't because God won't heal you until you trust Him; it's because your lack of trust undermines your faith and prevents you from receiving the healing that God has *already* provided for you.

In terms of trusting God, you have to start where you are. You have to be able to lift five pounds before you can lift one hundred. If you can't trust God in the area of your finances, Satan will use the fear you are embracing to stop your physical healing. It isn't that God won't bless you; it's that Satan is stealing from you because you haven't obeyed God.

Whoever you yield yourself to as a servant will rule over you—whether you obey sin and fear, which leads to death, or give obedience to righteousness and the Word of God, which leads to life. Yielding to fear, greed, or selfishness in your life is the same as yielding to Satan, who is the author of those things. Yielding to Satan allows him to hinder you from receiving from God. It can stop your healing, it can stop your marriage from working, it can stop any number of things because you aren't trusting God.

On the other hand, trusting God empowers Him to move in your life. Blinders fall from your eyes and you begin to get revelation from the Word like never before. You will start experiencing God's supernatural supply for your needs, causing you to trust God even more. Fear empowers the enemy; faith empowers God.

Obeying God is important. Giving money to support the Gospel is just one example of how obeying, or failing to obey, affects other areas of your life. The same is true in the area of husbands loving their wives, wives respecting their husbands, assembling together with other believers, and on and on we could go. Failing to obey God in areas where He has already given you direction gives Satan an inroad into your life.

Satan did not originally have authority to oppress the earth. God gave dominion over the earth to Adam and Eve (Genesis 1:26-28). They turned over their authority to Satan when they were tempted and gave in to him. We empower the devil by our actions in exactly the same way. Satan is powerless on his own. He needs physical human beings to yield to him and empower him.

Actions are linked to obedience. We release the power of God by acting on what He has told us to do. We release the power of the devil through our wrong actions, or lack of action. When God tells us to do something and we don't do it, we yield ourselves to Satan, the author of the fear or temptation that is keeping us from obeying God. When we yield to Satan, it empowers him to wreak havoc in our lives.

Sexual purity is an area that seems to trip a lot of people up. I've heard about unmarried couples who are living together, while trying to use God's grace as an excuse for living in sin. It's true that God loves them; He's not mad at them and He isn't going to punish them. God loves us whether we are married and living a godly life or not. It may offend some people to hear that, but it's true.

Jesus ministered to a woman living under the same circumstances. He showed her love and offered to give her living water (John 4:1-26). God isn't mad at you if you aren't married to the person you are shacking up with, but your disobedience is giving Satan an inroad into your life. The Lord didn't tell us that we were supposed to be united to one person in marriage because He is a spoilsport. He did it because He knows what is best for us. God knows how divorce and broken relationships hurt people. He also knows what makes us happy.

God created Adam and Eve, not Adam and Steve. God said that it's not good for a man to be alone, so he made a woman— not another man. God's plan is for us to live in heterosexual relationships, but He loves homosexuals too. The grace of God applies to everyone. He's not mad at people for living a gay lifestyle. God loves homosexuals, but living that way gives Satan a huge inroad into their life.

Anyone who wants to fulfill God's will doesn't have the luxury of giving Satan access to their life. The enemy is out to kill you. He is out to destroy your life and stop you from fulfilling God's will. Intentionally failing to do what God has directed you to do, through the Bible or otherwise, is like walking up to Satan and telling him to take his best shot. When Satan cleans your clock, don't go to God and ask Him why He let it happen. He didn't let it happen—*you* let it happen. You gave Satan free access. You gave him an inroad into your life. You can't live in sin and prosper. Sooner or later, it's going to catch up with you.

God doesn't turn away from us because of sin or imperfection. If He did, He would have turned away from the entire human race, because none of us are perfect (Romans 3:23). God doesn't change the way He relates to us according to our behavior; His grace is always the same. But Satan is out to hinder us. We can't let Satan come into our life, encumber us with all sorts of weight, and still win the race. It doesn't work that way. We need to obey God if we want to finish our race.

Saving Faith

> *What doth it profit, my brethren, though a man say he hath*
> *faith, and have not works? Can faith save him? ... faith, if it*
> *hath not works, is dead, being alone.*

> *James 2:14,17*

Scripture says that we are saved by grace through faith (Ephesians 2:8), so faith does save. Yet, this scripture is asking whether faith can save a man who doesn't have works. The point here is that faith is never alone. Saving faith is always accompanied by action. If someone runs into a crowded movie theater and shouts "Fire!", there will be some accompanying action. Everyone who really believes there is a fire is going to act. Some people might faint, some might scream, others might panic or run, but everyone who believes that there's a fire is going to do something.

Anyone who says, "I believe," but doesn't act on it, doesn't really believe. If you really believe God is your source, then you will give from your resources. If you trust God there will be evidence of it in your life. Your actions reveal what you truly believe. Faith alone saves, but saving faith is never alone. It causes action. Your actions are vital to your faith. James went on to say,

> *Yea, a man may say, Thou hast faith, and I have works: shew*
> *me thy faith without thy works, and I will shew thee my faith*
> *by my works. Thou believest that there is one God; thou doest*
> *well: the devils also believe, and tremble.*

> *James 2:18-19*

This is one of the most sarcastic statements in the entire Bible. You believe that there is one God? Good, but you haven't done anything the devil hasn't done. The devil believes, to the point that he trembles, but his actions don't correspond to faith. Satan knows that God exists but his actions are against God.

But wilt thou know, O vain man, that faith without works is dead?

James 2:20

The devil believes but his works are against God, therefore he doesn't have saving faith. People can say, "Oh, I believe God exists," but if their actions are contrary to the Lord's direction then they 'aren't believing with "saving faith". They only have mental assent. Faith without corresponding action is not true faith.

During the time that Jamie and I were struggling financially, I painted houses for a little while to make ends meet. One day I felt sick so I went home during my lunch break. I was so sick I couldn't even sit up. I was scheduled to get paid that day, so I needed to go back and finish work, but I only felt like lying down and taking a nap.

"You can't stay home today," Jamie said to me. "We need this money."

So Jamie prayed for me to be healed. I still felt bad though, so I started to lie back down on the couch and Jamie said, "Oh, no you're not. You are *not* going to act sick." She put her arm around me, stood me up, and walked me all through the house dancing and jumping. At first, she was dancing and I was being dragged around. I was praying for healing, but I wanted to act sick because that's how I felt. Jamie made me start acting like I was healed. By the end of my lunch break, I felt totally normal. I went back to work that afternoon and I got paid. But I didn't feel well until I started *acting* well.

Faith doesn't reach completion until we begin to act in accordance with what we profess to believe; action must be joined together with belief. We can't just quit taking medicine, thinking the action of stopping our medicine is going to make us well. People die doing foolish things like that. The Bible says with the heart man believes and with the mouth confession is made (Romans 10:10). First we have to believe in our heart that God has healed us *then* we can act on what we believe. If we believe with our heart and confess with our mouth, we will see it come to pass. *Actions follow faith—they don't generate faith.* Faith has to come first. We believe with our heart and our faith will be made perfect as we begin to act on what we believe.

Taking Responsibility

Many Christians are more dominated by their emotions than by what they believe. They let their feelings control how they act, instead of letting faith steer them. Seeing God's will fulfilled in your life means learning to obey Him no matter how you feel. After you have heard God's direction and learned how to follow His will, you have to learn to be obedient to see His will fulfilled in your life. I highly recommend that you obey God in every area of your life, even if you feel like you simply can't do what God is leading you to do. Trust God and follow His leading. He will never lead you to do something you can't do or something that isn't in your best interest.

You can always do what God is asking you to do. You may lack the motivation but you *can* do it if you really want to. Several years ago, my nephew came to me after he had received two or three speeding tickets and was about to have his license revoked.

"I can't help it," he said. "I just drive fast."

"That's not true," I told him. "You can help it."

"No, honest, I can't," he replied.

"If I was to sit in the back seat of your car with a gun pointed at your head and threatened to pull the trigger the moment you go over 55 miles an hour, could you drive less than 55?" I asked.

"Well, yeah, I guess," he said.

"See," I said, "you can do it. You just lack the motivation."

Modern society tends to avoid responsibility at all costs. Our culture is always trying to shift the blame onto someone else or some exterior circumstance, anything other than accepting responsibility ourselves. People have a tendency to excuse all kinds of behavior because no one wants to be responsible for their actions. The real culprit, we're told, is the dysfunctional household we were raised in, our hormones, or because we are middle aged, or a teenager. The truth is there are always reasons why we are the way we are, but there are no excuses.

To fulfill God's will, you have to accept responsibility in your life. You aren't an evolved animal simply responding to stimuli. You are a person created in the image of God, therefore you are responsible for your actions. Quit blaming other people for your current situation. Maybe some terrible things happened to you in the past, but you can accept responsibility for any wrong choices you have made in response and move on with your life. As long as you play the role of a victim, you will never be a victor.

God commanded us: "rejoice in the Lord always: and again I say, Rejoice" (Phil 4:4). I believe the reason He said "and *again* I say rejoice" is because He knew people were going to think, "He couldn't possibly have meant *always*." Regardless of what you are going through, God says you can rejoice. It doesn't matter if you're going through a divorce, someone close to you has died, or if some other tragedy has struck your life. God would be unjust to command you to "rejoice in the Lord always" if it wasn't possible.

Jesus said, "In the world ye shall have tribulation: but be of good cheer; I have overcome the world" (John 16:33). He admitted that we are going to have problems, but He told us to be of good cheer. The word "rejoice" is a verb; it's an action, not something you possess. You don't have to feel joy to rejoice in the Lord because you always have joy in your spirit, whether you can feel it or not (Galatians 5:22). You can rejoice through gritted teeth or with tears running down your face.

We can do what God tells us to do regardless of how we feel. Once we start obeying God, we will discover that we have a well on the inside of us that is full of the life of God. Rejoicing is like putting a bucket down into the well of life in our spirit and drawing out the fullness of God. We may start rejoicing through gritted teeth, but if we keep rejoicing we will draw out the life of God that's inside of us. We will experience *real* joy and peace. We can't be led through life by our emotions. We have to be led by the Spirit of God.

One thing that distinguishes an adult from a child is the fact that adults try not to base their decisions on how they feel. As adults, we don't always feel like going to work, but we do it because we know we need to. We don't always feel like being the parent; sometimes we want to be the child and want to fall down on the floor, throw a fit, and shout, "I didn't ask for this!" But when you're a parent, you know you need to be responsible and act like it. Yet, when it comes to our emotions, we don't take control. Most of us let emotions dominate our lives and dictate our behavior. Emotions should be like the caboose on a train—going wherever the train goes,—but not determining anything.

Sometimes I don't feel like praying for people. When I first started in ministry, I didn't think God was doing anything unless I had a tingling sensation shooting up and down my spine. Praise God, I had enough sense to keep my mouth shut. I simply kept praying over people and believing that, as the Bible says, when Christians lay hands on the sick, they will recover. So I just kept praying for people. Soon I discovered that I saw some of the greatest miracles when I felt absolutely nothing as I prayed. Those experiences helped me learn not to be led by my feelings.

A Place Called There

And Elijah the Tishbite, who was of the inhabitants of Gilead, said unto Ahab, As the LORD God of Israel liveth, before whom I stand, there shall not be dew nor rain these years, but according to my word.

1 Kings 17:1

Elijah received a word from God and acted on it. You have to understand the historical background to fully appreciate this story. Ahab and his wife, Jezebel, had outlawed the worship of God and were killing all of God's prophets. Elijah was putting his life on the line to deliver a prophecy to Ahab. He could have focused on the dangers to himself, but instead he was obedient to the Lord. He received a word from God and *acted* on it.

Ahab knew that Elijah had prophesied the drought, so when it came he searched every nation and kingdom to find Elijah (1 Kings 18:10). Three and a half years later, Elijah finally showed himself to Ahab and instructed him to gather all of the false prophets of Baal together in one place. The king obeyed; he was actually taking orders from Elijah.

Elijah became the most dominant man in the entire nation because he received direction from God and acted on it. If he would have stayed in his prayer closet and prayed for a drought without confronting Ahab, the king would never have obeyed him and Elijah wouldn't have initiated the greatest revival Israel had ever seen.

Immediately after Elijah prophesied the drought, God gave him further direction:

Get thee hence, and turn thee eastward, and hide thyself by the brook Cherith, that is before Jordan. And it shall be, that thou shalt drink of the brook; and I have commanded the ravens to feed thee there. So he went and did according unto the word of the LORD...

1 Kings 17:2-5

God gave Elijah a promise of protection, but notice that the promise to provide for Elijah didn't come until *after* he obeyed God's first instruction. This is why so many people don't fulfill God's will for their lives. God reveals His will, but people start trying to rationalize how everything is going to work out before they act on what He has told them to do. God didn't make provision for Elijah until *after* he acted on the first thing God told him to do. I made this same point earlier: God won't show you steps two through ten until you obey step one.

After Elijah obeyed the first thing God told him to do, God said, "Now go to the brook Cherith, I have commanded the ravens to feed you *there*." God sent Elijah's provision *there*—not where Elijah was, but where God told him to go. Also, notice that God had already commanded the provision. This is similar to how a quarterback throws the football to the receiver. He doesn't throw the ball to where the receiver is when the ball is leaving his hand; he throws it where receiver is going to be when the ball gets there. He throws the ball out in front of the receiver.

Likewise, God doesn't send your provision to you; He sends your provision to where He told you to *go*. God might lead you to start a business or step out in faith and begin a new path. Wherever God might lead you, you won't see the provision where you are now, you will see it *there*—after you act on what He told you to do. You can't make following God's leading conditional upon seeing His provision first. God already sent His provision; it's on the way to where He told you to go or it's already waiting there for you. One reason you might not be seeing God's provision in your life is because you are too much *here*, and not enough *there*.

When God provided the $3.2 million we needed to renovate our building, He told me not to take out a loan but to trust Him for another way. After I obligated myself to see the provision come through my ministry partners, God sent His provision. When I made the decision to build debt-free, my accounting books indicated that it would take a hundred years to save that amount of money. However, after I acted on what God told me to do, He supplied the money in fourteen months!

Today, our ministry has taken a $50 million step of faith. Some people might think it's crazy to do that, but God told us to go there, so we're going. Our provision is *there*, and the closer we get to where God is telling us to go, the more of His provision we will see. We are building a brand new facility for Charis Bible College that will prepare thousands of believers to go out and make disciples of every nation. It's God's plan so He will bring it to pass.

By acting on God's direction, Elijah saw the greatest revival that had ever happened until that time. He didn't know how God was going to protect and provide for him until *after* he obeyed the first word God gave him. Many born-again, Spirit-filled believers look at their lives and only see problems. They don't understand that they have the same power on the inside of them that raised Jesus Christ from the dead (Ephesians 1:18-20). God's power isn't out in heaven someplace—it's on the inside of us.

We need to act on the instruction God has given us. For instance, the Bible says that speaking in tongues is rest and refreshing (Isaiah 28:12). So if you are discouraged and need to be refreshed, speak in tongues. I guarantee it will get you fired up. Instead of looking for a "fresh" word from God to fix your problem, act on the direction He has already given you in Scripture.

Every time we hear a word from God but fail to obey it, our heart becomes hardened. A hard heart develops the same way as a callus on our hand. It doesn't happen all at once; it forms one layer at a time. This is how we become calloused or insensitive to God. Every time God leads us to do something and we don't obey, it decreases our sensitivity by one layer. If we ignore God's leading enough, we will eventually think we can't hear His voice anymore. Even though our heart may become hardened, God will never stop speaking to us. Jesus said, "My sheep hear my voice, and I know them, and they follow me" (John 10:27). The Lord is always leading us and giving us instruction, but we need to be sensitive to it and act on it.

You may not have the tenth step of God's plan yet, but you know step one. God has put something on your heart. I'm sure there are reasons why you haven't followed through on whatever He has told you to do, but whatever the reasons are, they aren't good enough. God loves you whether you follow His leading or not. Being obedient doesn't make God love you more; failing to obey doesn't make Him love you less. But God can't lead and direct you into His blessings and fulfillment without your cooperation.

Once He tells you to do something and gives you direction, you need to act on it. God has given you everything you need to live a victorious life and see His will fulfilled in your life (2 Peter 1:3-4). You simply need to act on His Word and His leading.

Chapter 12

Patient Endurance

In our culture, we want what we want and we want it *right* now. Most people are so short term in their thinking that they go for the immediate fix in every situation. The average person is in debt up to his eyeballs because he buys things on borrowed time, without considering the long-term consequences. Rather than buying a used car that would meet a person's needs, he goes out and buys a brand new expensive car, which ends up costing two and a half times the original price tag after paying six years of interest! It all boils down to impatience. People are unwilling to wait and save money. They have to satisfy their cravings immediately. Even in the spiritual realm, very few people have patience.

The human tendency is to quit, fail, and give up. People can't wait. It's not human nature to wait. The strongest, best, and most fit of all are going to fail. In our own selves, we don't have what it takes to overcome. God, on the other hand, doesn't get weary. God doesn't faint. He never gives up. Patience is a God quality, not a human quality. Only through God can we obtain patience and endurance.

He giveth power to the faint; and to them that have no might he increaseth strength. Even the youths shall faint and be weary, and the young men shall utterly fall: But they that wait upon the LORD shall renew their strength; they shall mount up with wings as eagles; they shall run, and not be weary; and they shall walk, and not faint.

Isaiah 40:29-31

The verse says, "they that wait upon the Lord shall renew their strength." This isn't talking about waiting, like hanging around waiting for a bus or a train. Waiting on the Lord is more than just killing time until something happens. It's more like a waiter at a good restaurant: he watches to see if you need anything. "Can I get you more water? Is there anything else I can help you with?" This is exactly how we need to wait upon the Lord: watching, looking, and searching for ways to help. In order to fulfill God's purposes, we need Him to work His patience on the inside of us. We need God's ability to endure, because it is not human nature to be patient or persistent. We hate waiting and we're prone to give up when things get tough.

Sometimes when I teach this at Charis Bible College, people get upset. Some people have the attitude that they don't need to wait because they think God is going to do things for them instantly. Some have quit school before they graduate because they were so adamant about needing to do something *right now*. In most cases, years and years have passed and they still haven't done anything. They would have been better off to be patient and let God work in their lives to prepare them.

Even if someone finds God's will and starts following it, the likelihood that they will stick with it for a prolonged period of time is slim. I have seen this happen with ministers and people in every walk of life. I have seen so many people come and go, who initially had a zeal for God, but they couldn't maintain it. The Christian life is a marathon, not a sprint. Some people start the race well, pulling out ahead early, but they don't have any endurance. They stand for a short while but then they give up. This is a major problem in the body of Christ.

Resist Problems

I believe there has been a lot of wrong teaching about how to gain patience and endure in the Christian walk. Many preachers are teaching that tribulation and hardship will teach you patience. Often they will quote the scripture which says that tribulation *works* patience (Romans 5:3), but that scripture means work in the sense of "exercise." Tribulation does not *create* patience.

If hardship made people patient, then those who have suffered the most hardship would automatically be the most patient. But this isn't the case. Often the people who have the most problems are the least patient people you will ever meet. Patience doesn't come from problems. Tribulation only gives you the opportunity to grow and exercise patience.

Patience is simply faith over a prolonged period of time. Momentary faith is something you can build up in a person by encouraging them; patience is long-term faith that doesn't waiver. It stays consistent over a prolonged period of time. Plenty of people feel faith when they first get started walking with God, but they can't seem to maintain it.

The fruit of the Spirit is love, joy, peace, longsuffering, gentleness, goodness, faith, meekness, and temperance (Galatians 5:22). Longsuffering means patience—patience is actually a fruit of the Holy Spirit. When you are born again, God gives you patience, but you have to do something to activate it. Scripture says that faith comes by hearing and hearing by the Word of God (Rom 10:17). Patience is built up within you as you study the Word of God.

When pressure situations or trials come against you, they give you an opportunity to grow and develop in your faith, but faith must already be in you through the Word and through what God has put in your heart. Embracing problems is not going to help you. You have to resist problems. The teaching says that God puts problems in your life to make you patient or stronger is completely wrong. Satan puts problems in your life to steal the Word (Mark 4:16-17). But if you stand on the Word in the midst of your problems and keep doing what God tells you to do, you will become stronger in faith and patience. This is the manner in which tribulation *works* patience. Patience is important in the Christian walk, but it doesn't come through hardship—it comes through the Word of God (Romans 15:4).

Keep at It

And we desire that every one of you do shew the same diligence to the full assurance of hope unto the end: That ye be not slothful, but followers of them who through faith and patience inherit the promises.

Hebrews 6:11-12

In contrast to being slothful or lazy, we are encouraged to be followers of those who by faith and patience inherit the promises. Faith and patience take a lot of effort. You have to seek God. You have to be proactive about turning off other things that draw your attention away and numb you to God. It takes commitment. This is one of the reasons that coming to Bible school is so important for a lot of people—it's a major commitment. It costs money, effort, and a couple years of your life. When you put effort into something, you get more out of it.

Countless people's lives consist of getting up, going to work, coming home, watching television, going to bed, and then doing the whole thing all over again the next day—like a little hamster on a wheel going around and around. They aren't seeking God; they don't know what His Word says. They're getting nowhere in fulfilling His purpose for their lives. Inheriting the promises takes effort. You have to make a commitment to seek God.

Remaining constant is also important. We can't go in spurts, seeking the Lord when trouble is staring us in the face and then going back to carnal living as soon as the pressure is off. Carnal living is what produces problems in the first place! Living for God is the solution, but it takes effort on our part.

Nature tends toward a state of decline. It's easier to be fat than it is to stay skinny. It's easier to be sick than it is to get well. It's easier to float downstream than it is to swim upstream. We have to fight against the problems and sicknesses that try to come against us in life. A lot of people think they don't have any control over these things, but they do. *You* resist the devil, and he will flee from *you* (James 4:7).

Arthritis doesn't come on you all at once like a seizure. You don't wake up one morning and, *boom*, you have "full-blown" arthritis. It comes one little joint at a time. At first you accept it because it is only a little stiffness in one joint; you can live with that. You let it in, bit by bit, and before you know it, arthritis has riddled your entire body. That's exactly how sin works'. That's how the devil operates. He sneaks up on us little by little, bit by bit, temptation by temptation. It takes diligence for us to have the faith and patience necessary to resist the attacks of the enemy and stay in the Word of God.

Abraham had to patiently endure in order to inherit the promise God made to him. God made a promise to Abraham that he would be the father of many nations. Abraham had faith in what he heard. Faith comes by hearing and hearing by the Word of God (Romans 10:17). Abraham had a promise that he anchored his faith to, and after he had patiently endured, he obtained the promise (Hebrews 6:13-15). But it took a long time. Abraham was about 86 years old when God promised him that his descendants would outnumber the stars in the sky (Genesis 15:4-5), but his son Isaac wasn't born until he was 100 (Genesis 21:5). How many of us would have waited on a promise that long? Most people think God didn't come through for them unless something happens within the first five seconds of praying.

We need to realize that it often takes time to see God's will come to pass, especially outside of healing and other areas when an immediate miracle is needed. Trying to find and fulfill God's will for your life is a process. God can't take you from where you are to where you are supposed to be all in one step.

The Lord spoke to me on July 26, 1999, and told me I was just beginning my ministry. Wow! That was discouraging and encouraging all at the same time. I started ministering in 1968. I was 31 years into ministry when the Lord said I was just beginning. He said if I had died or stopped before going on TV on January 3, 2000, I would have missed my ministry. It's not that I had been out of the will of God; I had just been in preparation for 31 years. I was just entering into His perfect will (Romans 12:2).

The Lord spoke to me on January 31, 2002, and told me I was limiting Him by my small thinking. When I changed my thinking, the results were miraculous. We had about 30 employees at the time, now we have over 230. At that time, we were reaching six percent or less of the United States with our *Gospel Truth* television program; now we have the potential of reaching one hundred percent. More than two billion people around the world are able to watch our program. This all started happening more than 30 years *after* I entered into ministry. I'm fulfilling God's will step by step. It takes time so we need to have patience to not give up along the way.

Look Unto Jesus

> *Wherefore seeing we also are compassed about with so great a cloud of witnesses, let us lay aside every weight, and the sin which doth so easily beset us, and let us run with patience the race that is set before us, Looking unto Jesus the author and finisher of our faith; who for the joy that was set before him endured the cross, despising the shame, and is set down at the right hand of the throne of God.*
>
> *Hebrews 12:1-2*

Patience will keep us going day after day and year after year. It's how we endure. We get it by looking unto Jesus, the author and the finisher of our faith. Patience is a fruit of the Spirit (Galatians 5:22). It comes through the Word of God (Romans 15:4). Jesus is the Word of God (John 1:1) both living and written, therefore patience comes through a personal relationship with God. This amplifies another problem in many believers' lives: they honestly don't have a vibrant, life-giving relationship with Jesus. They know Him from a distance. When we have a good relationship with Jesus, not only do we talk to Him, but we also hear His voice when He speaks to us.

A great example of the importance of staying focused on Jesus is given in the Gospel of Matthew when Peter walked on water (Matthew 14:22-33). The disciples were out in a boat, in the middle of a large body of water, in rough seas, when Jesus came walking to them on the water. Peter said, "Lord, if it's you, bid me come unto you on the water." Jesus said, "Come." So Peter got out of the boat and started walking on the water. It was miraculous.

But after walking a little way, Peter took his eyes off of Jesus and started paying attention to the wind and the waves. When he did this, he began to sink. Think about that for a moment. The wind and the waves had absolutely nothing to do with Peter's ability to walk on water! He couldn't have walked on water even if the sea had been smooth as glass. The weather had nothing to do with it. Peter took his attention off of Jesus, the author and the finisher of his faith, and started focusing on his circumstances. When he did this, he began to sink.

It is notable that Peter didn't sink all at once. He just *began* to sink. In the same way, we don't lose our faith all at once. We don't get impatient all at once; it happens gradually. It is usually so gradual that we don't even realize we are taking our attention off of Jesus and looking at other things. We seek Jesus when our situation is impossible and we absolutely must have a miracle, but when things are going good we take our attention off of Him. We relax. That's when we get into trouble. Scripture goes on to tell us how to avoid this downfall.

For consider him that endured such contradiction of sinners against himself, lest ye be wearied and faint in your minds.

Hebrews 12:3

Fainting—the loss of strength or enthusiasm—begins in the mind. This is where the "sinking" begins. We have to guard our thoughts because Satan comes to us through our thinking. As a man thinks in his heart, so is he (Proverbs 23:7). We have to focus our thoughts and attention on Jesus. The sad fact is that most of us have allowed the cares of this life, the deceitfulness of riches, and the lust of other things to turn our attention away from the Lord and choke out His power in our lives (Mark 4:19). The reason we don't have patience is because we are focusing on the world and the instant gratification it offers. We aren't looking to the Lord.

If this is a problem for you, then the solution is simple: focus on Jesus, not your circumstances. Seek God with your whole heart. Keep your relationship with Him strong and you will endure. I have a course that I teach in our Bible school entitled "Longevity in Ministry," which focuses on maintaining a vibrant relationship with God. Fulfilling God's will is all about relationship. If you keep your relationship with God "red-hot," you will endure. You won't understand everything and you'll make some mistakes, but God will always show you the way to go when you are in relationship with Him.

Many seek what God has to offer, but they don't seek God Himself. When they are in a crisis, they seek Him. But when things are going good, they take their eyes off of Jesus and begin to sink. Our goal should be to seek a relationship with God first, then everything else will be given to us.

Pride and Circumstances

Earlier, I used Elijah as an example of someone who heard a word from God and acted on it. God did some truly great miracles through him because he was willing to be obedient. Elijah prophesied to King Ahab that there would be a drought, and then disappeared for three years (1 Kings 17:1). When Elijah returned, he told Ahab to gather the entire nation of Israel together at Mount Carmel for a contest: four hundred prophets of the grove and four hundred fifty prophets of Baal would "face-off" against Elijah (1 Kings 18:17-40). Elijah directed that they would each prepare an ox for sacrifice and then call for it to be consumed by fire. Then the true God would reveal Himself by sending fire from heaven to consume the sacrifice.

The prophets of the grove and the prophets of Baal called for fire from morning until late in the day, but nothing happened. While they were busy crying out to their false gods, Elijah mocked them saying, "Maybe your god is talking to someone else, or he is on a journey, or maybe he's taking a nap and you should wake him." The false prophets became so desperate, they started cutting themselves.

When nothing happened by late afternoon, Elijah called for the people to draw near as he prepared his sacrifice. He built an altar out of twelve stones and then dug a trench around it. When the altar was built and the sacrifice was in place, he ordered the people to pour twelve barrels of water over the sacrifice and wood. Water soaked through the sacrifice, drenched the wood, and overflowed into the trenches Elijah had dug. Then Elijah called upon God to consume the sacrifice with fire. The Lord sent a fire from heaven that was so hot it consumed the sacrifice, the wood, and the stone altar as well. When the people saw the consuming fire, they fell on their faces and said, "The Lord, he is the God; the Lord, he is the God." Elijah had the people detain the false prophets, then he killed them.

After all that, Elijah told Ahab to eat and drink because he could hear the sound of an abundance of rain. Then he went to the top of Mount Carmel to pray. The three-year drought was about to end. He prayed seven times and finally a cloud the size of a man's hand appeared on the horizon. When that tiny cloud appeared, Elijah sent word to Ahab to prepare his chariot and head for home before he got stopped by the coming downpour. Shortly after Ahab departed, the drought was broken by a deluge. Elijah started running on foot to the same city and actually outran Ahab's chariot to their destination (1 Kings 18:41-46). Elijah was pumped; his adrenalin was flowing.

Ahab's wife, Jezebel, was furious that Elijah had killed all of her false prophets. She sent a message to Elijah that said, "So let the gods do to me, and more also, if I make not thy life as the life of one of them by tomorrow about this time" (1 Kings 19:2). When Elijah saw this, he ran for his life. I don't doubt that Jezebel hated Elijah, but she was blowing smoke. She was threatening something that she couldn't follow through with. Even tyrants have to consider the will of the people. The entire nation had seen fire fall from heaven at Elijah's word, so they wouldn't have let her kill Elijah.

If Jezebel had felt free to kill Elijah, she would have sent a soldier with a sword instead of a messenger with a note. She wanted Elijah dead, but she couldn't kill him. Her note was just intimidation, which is exactly how the devil gets to us. He has no power over us, so he intimidates us. Then we defeat ourselves by running off in unbelief.

Jezebel said she was going to make Elijah like one of the 850 false prophets he had killed. Praise God, we live under a better covenant and God doesn't deal with people like that anymore. But imagine what the scene looked like where Elijah killed 850 people. It must have been a gruesome picture. The scripture says that when Elijah "saw" what Jezebel said to him, he ran. Her note brought the gruesome image to his mind and he saw himself as one of the men he had just slain. He saw himself as a dead man. He had just challenged the king and an entire nation, called down fire from heaven, and outrun a chariot. Now he was running from a woman with a note.

The Bible says that Elijah ran a day's journey into the wilderness, sat down under a juniper tree, and asked God to take his life. He said, "It is enough; now, O LORD, take away my life; for I am not better than my fathers" (1 Kings 19:4). Elijah's request reveals a lot. He wanted God to kill him because he said, "I am not better than my fathers." He suddenly came to the conclusion that he wasn't any better than his forefathers and it drove him into despair. This means that *prior* to this incident, he thought he *was* better than his forefathers.

Elijah had a string of unbroken successes. God protected him from Ahab during the three year drought and supplied his needs supernaturally during that time. Elijah was the first man recorded in the Bible to see a person raised from the dead (1 Kings 17:19-23). I know fifty or sixty people who have been raised from the dead. It's a relatively common thing today, but back then nobody had ever even heard of such a thing. Elijah was a powerful man of God. The problem was he started to believe he was someone special. He took his eyes off of God and began thinking it was his own power and ability that was making all of these miraculous things possible.

This story illustrates the point I'm making: you have to look unto Jesus, the author and the finisher of your faith. You have to keep your attention on Him. Proverbs says that pride goes before destruction, and a haughty spirit before a fall (Proverbs 16:18). The moment you start patting yourself on the back and believing your own press releases, you are in trouble. It doesn't matter what you accomplish; you are still only a man or a woman.

It's like being in an airplane. People say, "I'm flying 500 miles an hour at 30,000 feet." No, you're not. The plane is flying; you're not. It's your position inside of the plane that keeps you airborne. If you don't believe it, then step outside of the plane and see what happens. You will plummet like a rock. In the same way, Christians aren't changing unbelievers' lives and causing miracles to happen. You aren't doing those things; God living in you is doing them. And if you ever take your attention off Jesus, the author and the finisher of your faith, you are headed for a fall.

Elijah didn't have the patience to endure in this situation because he got caught up in pride. Success ruined him. The same thing happens to us today. Not many people continue to seek God on the other side of a crisis, when everything is fine and their needs are met. As soon as they get whatever they were praying for, they go back to doing their own thing and begin the process of sinking all over again.

If you aren't careful, the circumstances of life will cause you to take your eyes off of Jesus. For example, if somebody dies, all of a sudden, you take your attention off of Jesus and begin to focus on your pain. As you do, you begin to sink. If your business fails and the financial pressure gets to you and you take your eyes off of Jesus as the Provider of all your needs, you will begin to sink.

Patience is the ability to fix your attention on Jesus, not looking to the right hand or to the left. It's the ability to remain unmoved by your circumstances. The only way I know how to get this kind of patience is by maintaining a close relationship with God through the Word. This sort of watchful vigilance is what it means to "wait upon the Lord."

It doesn't matter if it has been ten years since God gave you major direction or if you are healthy and crisis free, stay focused on

Jesus. God isn't going to speak life-changing words to you every day. He tells you He loves you and He gives you guidance, but He doesn't give you life-altering direction every day. Long stretches of time may pass when you are just studying the Word and doing what God told you to do last. That's okay; *patience* is faith over a prolonged period of time. Just do what God told you to do until He tells you differently.

Facing Adversity

After Elijah fell into pride, God tried to raise him up in the same way Jesus reached out his hand to Peter. He sent Elijah on a 40-day journey to Mount Horeb. When Elijah arrived there, he hid in a cave and the voice of the Lord asked him, "What are you doing here Elijah?" Instead of running away from Jezebel to hide in the wilderness, Elijah should have been leading the nation of Israel in the revival he started when he called down fire and killed the false prophets.

Elijah answered, "I have been very jealous for the LORD God of hosts: for the children of Israel have forsaken thy covenant, thrown down thine altars, and slain thy prophets with the sword; and I, even I only, am left; and they seek my life, to take it away" (1 Kings 19:10). Elijah got caught up in self-pity and said something he knew was a lie. Right before Elijah told the king to assemble Israel before Mount Carmel, he met a man who had hidden 100 prophets of God and was keeping them safe (1 Kings 18:13). Elijah knew that he wasn't the only prophet left alive.

This is what happens when you focus on your circumstances. You know things aren't really as bad as you think they are, but you get so focused on the problem that it becomes overwhelming. One person may wrong you and you start complaining that nobody loves you and everything is going wrong. But that's not true and you know it; it's how you feel so you indulge your flesh and start feeling sorry for yourself. You are headed for trouble once you start down that road. You need to get a grip on reality. You have to put things into perspective. Stop focusing on your problems and start focusing on God. Jesus is the same yesterday, today, and forever. He doesn't change. If your life is based on Jesus, you will be happy when circumstances look bad and you will be blessed when things look good. It won't matter either way; you will be consistent.

Elijah was way out of perspective so God told him to go out and stand at the opening of the cave as He passed by. Three dramatic manifestations followed. A wind passed by that was so strong it broke the rocks, but the Lord was not in the wind. After the wind, there came an earthquake, but the Lord was not in the earthquake. After the earthquake was a fire, but God was not in the fire either. Finally, Elijah heard a still small voice and it overwhelmed him so much that he wrapped his face in his cloak and went to stand at the opening of the cave (1 Kings 19:11-13). Some people miss God because they look for Him in the spectacular, but God delights in faith and we need to be listening for Him in the still small voice that is on the inside of us.

God asked Elijah, "What are you doing here?" This is the exact same question God asked him the first time (1 Kings 19:9). Here's a tip: if God asks you a question and you answer it, and then He asks you the exact same question again, it probably means you didn't get the answer right the first time. God is giving you a "do-over." Elijah didn't pick up on this, so he gave God the exact same answer. Elijah may have felt like the only prophet around, but he knew he wasn't. He was being dominated by his emotions. So God told him to return to Damascus, anoint Hazael king over Syria, Jehu king over Israel, and anoint Elisha to be prophet in his place (1 Kings 19:15-18). In other words, God told him to go find a replacement to carry on the ministry that He needed someone to complete since Elijah had given up.

Elijah only did one of the three things that God asked him to do. He anointed Elisha to replace him (1 Kings 19:19-21), but he didn't do the other two things he heard God tell him to do in an audible voice. We know this because Elisha was the one who anointed Hazael king over Syria and Jehu king over Israel (2 Kings 8:7-13 and 2 Kings 9:1-7).

Elijah checked out because he was depressed and discouraged. He didn't fulfill God's will for his life. Elijah was the first person to see someone raised from the dead (1 Kings 17:17-23) and food miraculously provided (1 Kings 17:10-16). He also called fire down out of heaven and turned an entire nation to God (1 Kings 18:38-39)! This is a prime example of how finishing is a lot harder than starting. Elijah did not fulfill God's purpose for his life because he lost his focus. He got caught up in pride and took his attention off of God, the author and the finisher of his faith. He quit operating in patience.

Elijah missed it big time, but God still loved him. We have a tendency to think that God gets mad when we fail because that's our experience in human relationships. But God doesn't operate that way. God didn't reject Elijah. In fact, Elijah's relationship with God was so strong that he never physically died. As Elijah and Elisha were walking together one day, a chariot with horses of fire swooped down and took Elijah up to heaven in a whirlwind (2 Kings 2:11). Elijah had such a strong relationship with God that he was one of two people who never physically died. (Enoch was the other one - Genesis 5:24). God supernaturally translated him up into heaven.

Elijah's failure to carry out all of the things God asked him to had consequences, but God didn't punish him. Ahab was supposed to be replaced as king by Jehu (1 Kings 19:16), but he wasn't replaced and terrible things happened as a result. Ahab killed Naboth (1 Kings 21), which wouldn't have happened if Jehu had been king. The nation of Israel was in dire straits because Elijah didn't obey God, but God wasn't mad at him.

Even if you don't do everything that God calls you to do, His grace will still abound toward you (Romans 5:20). God will still love you. You can still go to heaven without following God and doing everything He wants you to do. But our lives have a purpose. We have a job to do, and it isn't just about us being blessed. Who knows how things might have turned out if Elijah would have obeyed God instead of falling into self-pity? We don't know what tragedy could have been avoided or what miracles might have come through him.

I have heard estimates that 80% of ministers today quit within the first five years of entering full-time ministry. What could they have accomplished if they had finished their course instead? A large percentage of those who remain in ministry are depressed and discouraged. What would happen if they knew how to operate in patience and look unto Jesus, the author and the finisher of their faith? What would our world look like if every person who started the race was still in it and doing what God told them to do?

A lot of people start the race, but not many stay at it over the long haul. Finishing is more important than starting. You inherit the promises through faith and patience. You have to run with patience the race that is set before you, looking unto Jesus, not diverting your attention to the right hand or to the left. When you are running a race, you can't go up into the grandstands and argue with the spectators; you might win the argument, but you are going to lose the race. Stay on track. Keep doing what God told you to do. Stay focused on Jesus and don't get distracted by adverse circumstances in your life.

Make a commitment that you're going to love the Lord to the best of your ability. Determine now that you are going to keep running your race no matter what. Don't ever turn away from that commitment. Fulfilling God's will isn't for lazy Christians. You have to seek God with your whole heart, but it's worth it!

Chapter 13

Glorify the Lord

Because that which may be known of God is manifest in them;
for God hath shewed it unto them. For the invisible things
of him from the creation of the world are clearly seen, being
understood by the things that are made, even his eternal power
and Godhead; so that they are without excuse.

Romans 1:19-20

In this verse, the Apostle Paul is explaining that you don't have to tell people how unholy they are, they already know it. We all possess an intuitive knowledge that God is holy and we are not. It's true that some people have hardened their hearts by repeatedly turning away from God. They may say they have no conviction about living in sin, but in truth, God has revealed Himself to every human being and we all know in our hearts that sin is wrong.

The Bible says, "Be still and know that I am God" (Psalm 46:10). The reason people always want the television or music on or are constantly doing something is because they don't want to be still. If you are still and quiet, this little homing device that God placed on the inside of you starts going off, and asking, "Is this all there is to life?" Stillness brings an awareness of God; the world drowns this out with activity.

Our hearts speak to us 24 hours a day. Every minute of every day, God reveals Himself to us, but the noise of this world drowns out the still, small voice of God. We can deaden ourselves or get calloused to the voice of God, but God will never stop reaching out to us. We don't need someone to tell us that God exists. Every person on the planet at one time or another has known that God is real. After a while, we can become so accustomed to living out of our natural understanding that our heart becomes hardened and we don't remember ever knowing God. But really, everyone has known God is real from the time they were little.

In the Vietnam War, I saw people who claimed to be atheists cry out to God the minute bullets started flying and bombs began dropping. When crisis comes and the illusion of control is shattered, unbelievers cry out for God to save them because in their hearts they know He is real and that He can save them. I quit arguing with people about whether or not God exists. You can't argue a person into believing in God because by claiming not to believe in God, they are choosing to ignore all of the evidence around them.

The Bible says the things of God are clearly seen. Anyone who says they don't believe God exists is either lying, or they have hardened their heart to the truth. It's possible to push God far enough away or harden your heart to the extreme that you become a reprobate, which means that God takes all conviction away from you

(Romans 1:28). Nobody can come to the Father unless the Holy Spirit draws them (John 6:44), so you are damned if the Holy Spirit quits drawing you. Even at that point though, it doesn't mean you don't know that God exists, it just means that you are past feeling remorse for rebelling against Him.

Nobody will ever be able to stand before God and claim that His judgment isn't fair because they never knew He exists. Every person who has ever drawn a breath on this planet has known there's a God. Someone can harden himself to the point of rejecting God entirely, but it doesn't happen quickly. Generally, it takes time to become as numb to God as our society is today. Insensitivity to God is built up by countless denials of the simple witness of God in your heart, but it happens.

Staying Sensitive to God

Because that, when they knew God, they glorified him not as God, neither were thankful; but became vain in their imaginations, and their foolish heart was darkened.

Romans 1:21

This passage describes the progressive process in which our hearts can become hardened toward God. It shows the desensitization process that someone goes through. No one is going to fulfill God's will for their life by allowing their heart to become hardened toward Him. We need to avoid this downward spiral. I believe that if we do the opposite of the process described in this scripture, we will remain sensitive to God and avoid being desensitized.

This verse says that although they knew God, they didn't glorify Him as God. The Greek word used here for *glorify* means "to render or esteem glorious,"which is another way of saying to value, or to prize. In other words, they didn't value or prize the things of God. Satan will always try to get us to decrease the value, esteem, or worth that we place on the things of God. Unfortunately, the devil doesn't have to work very hard to entice most people down this path. We live in a carnal world and the things of God are not valued by the world. When we share the values of the world instead of God's values, the hardening process begins. The Lord's values are completely different from most of what the world values. The apostle John put it this way,

> *Love not the world, neither things that are in the world. If*
> *any man love the world, the love of the father is not in him.*
> *For all that is in the world, the lust of the flesh, and the lust*
> *of the eyes, and the pride of life, is not of the Father, but is of*
> *the world.*
>
> *1 John 2:15–16*

Christians watch the same junk on television that unbelievers watch. They read the same garbage and listen to the same ungodly music. The majority of Christians use the same things for entertainment as the world. Is it any wonder that the church is becoming more and more like the world? The world says that God is dead, He doesn't exist, and none of the miracles we see performed in the name of God are real. We can't share the world's values, without becoming desensitized to God. Whatever we focus our attention on is going to dominate us. The Holy Spirit draws us toward a more intimate relationship with God, while the world pulls us the other way.

I have seen people raised from the dead. I have seen blind eyes opened. I have seen every type of miracle you can imagine, and people say to me, "If those miracles are real, then why don't you put it on the nightly news for everyone to see? Why don't you verify all of the miracles you see?" I don't bother because there would be no point. The world doesn't believe in miracles. The world doesn't value the things of God so they cannot accept that miracles are real. Unbelievers would sit in front of their television and try to find a way to deny the report, hardening their hearts even more. They would see someone get up out of a wheelchair and say, "Well, she must not have been all that bad off to begin with."

Contrary to what some think, seeing is *not* believing. Neither does faith come by miracles. Faith comes by the Word of God (Romans 10:17). Miracles help those who already believe or want to believe but are struggling with doubt. Miracles help us remove doubt, but faith only comes through the Word of God.

People gathered at the tomb of Lazarus and saw Jesus raise him from the dead. They watched it with their own eyes (John 11:38-44). Lazarus had been dead and buried for several days. His body was already decaying. When Jesus told them to roll away the gravestone, Lazarus' sister protested that there would be an odor because he had already been dead four days. Lazarus was wrapped head to toe in grave clothes; both of his legs were wrapped together like a mummy, he couldn't walk. This means that when Jesus called him to "come forth," God supernaturally translated him to the opening of the cave.

Everyone standing there saw a corpse raised from the dead, but they didn't let it change what they believed. Some of them conspired to kill Jesus and Lazarus with him (John 11:45-53). If you have a heart to disbelieve, you won't believe even if you see someone raised from the dead, which is exactly what Jesus taught in the parable of the rich man (Luke 16:19-31). Jesus said that if people won't believe Moses and the prophets—the Word of God—they won't believe a miracle either.

You can have a tremendous experience with the Lord on Sunday, but when you go to your place of work on Monday, Satan is going to parade people by you who will try to devalue your experience. Whenever you make a commitment to God or something miraculous happens, you are going to have family, friends, work associates, or somebody laugh at you when you tell them what happened. They aren't going to appreciate your experience to the degree that you do. This is one way that Satan tries to change the value you place on the things of God. It is similar to the way a seesaw works: when your opinion of God is up, everyone else's opinion is going to be lower or of less significance. On the other hand, if you start accepting the values and views of people, your esteem for the things of God will decrease. It isn't possible to highly value both the opinion of man and the opinion of God at the same time.

Jesus said, "How can you believe, which receive honor from one of another, and seek not the honor that comes from God only?" (John 5:44). It is impossible to really believe God when you are a man-pleaser. Most people are co-dependent on the approval of others. They don't like being rejected or ridiculed, so they value the opinion of other people more than they value God's opinion. Proverbs says the fear of man brings a snare (Proverbs 29:25). Nobody likes rejection, but we can't be troubled by it because the first step to diminishing the impact of God in our life is to start worrying about what other people have to say.

The Bible says that all who live godly in Christ Jesus will suffer persecution (2 Timothy 3:12). You haven't been living a godly life for very long if you've never suffered persecution. If you never bump into the devil, it's because you and the devil are both heading in the same direction. When you turn around and start going against the flow, you are going to meet resistance. You will encounter persecution. If you are more concerned with the approval of people than you are with God, you will quit glorifying God. The moment you shift your value system to exalt the opinions of other people above God, your heart begins to harden.

A long time ago as I was hiking up Pike's Peak with a friend of mine, he began to talk about a guy who was very critical of us, a guy who was supposedly our friend. Whenever we were around him, he was sweet and everything was fine. But behind our backs, he constantly criticized us. My friend and I had discussed this situation before because it really bothered him. So, as we were hiking up Pike's Peak, he started telling me the latest thing that this pastor was saying about us behind our backs.

I said, "I don't want to hear it. I know this guy doesn't like us, but I just don't care." My friend started to say something in response, but then stopped. Finally he said, "Why don't the things he is saying bother you like it bothers me?"

I told him, "Because I don't value his opinion the way you do."

The only people who will ever let us down are the people we lean on. God will never let us down so we need to lean on Him. It's not that we don't care about other people; it's just that we shouldn't need them to pat us on the back in order to feel good about ourselves. We need to bask in the fact that our Heavenly Father loves us. Then when criticism comes, even though we don't like it, it won't keep us up at night. When we esteem God's opinion the highest, what other people have to say just won't matter all that much.

I experienced God's love in a huge way on March 23, 1968 and it transformed my life. I stood up on Sunday morning and told the whole church how God had changed me. I didn't know how to describe what had happened so I told them I was "filled with the Holy Spirit." Boy, they jumped on me like a chicken on a June bug! The pastor said to me, "Who do you think you are? The Apostle Paul was filled with the Spirit. Peter was filled with the Spirit. Are you saying you're like an apostle? Are you better than the rest of us?" I didn't mean anything by saying that I was filled with the Spirit; I was just trying to communicate what happened to me. But the people around me tried to devalue what God had done.

I was glorifying God. I was celebrating what He had done, and immediately an authority figure came along and tried to get me to value his opinion above God's by asking, "Who do you think you are?" In his eyes, I was just an 18-year-old kid, whereas he was a pastor who had been to seminary. He wanted me to value his opinion more. The youth leader of the church, the pastor of the church, friends, relatives, and everybody else told me that I was missing God.

All of those things were an attempt to get me to put greater worth on the opinion of men than on God. If I would have valued their opinion and started doubting what I felt in my heart, I would have quit glorifying God—and I would have taken the first step toward losing the fullness of joy and victory I received through my experience with the Lord. I didn't understand much back then, but by the grace of God, I just kept thinking, I *don't know what your problem is, but I know God has spoken to me.* I knew I had encountered God. All of the criticism that came rolled off me like water on a duck's back.

Shortly after I quit college, I became reclassified as "available for service" in the military draft system. Before I was drafted, a recruiter came to my house and explained the benefits of volunteering for service. He was dressed in his military uniform and did his best to project an authoritative presence. He sat down in my living room, spread all of his pamphlets out on the table, and started telling me how volunteering could keep me out of Vietnam. He was only part way into his spiel when I stopped him. "Look," I said, "I can save us both a lot of time."

"Really, how's that?" he asked.

I began to tell him my story, "The reason I was reclassified for the draft, and that you're here, is because I quit school and lost my student deferment."

"That's right" he said.

"But you see," I said, "God told me to quit school. So I'm following God. And if God wants me to be drafted then I'll be drafted, but if He doesn't, I won't."

The recruiter burst out in laughter. "Boy," he said, gasping for breath, "I can guarantee, you *are* going to Vietnam."

When he said that, something inside of me snapped. I was valuing God; His will was more important to me than anything else in my life. I believed God was all powerful. I was esteeming the things of God. Yet, in front of me was an authority figure who placed zero worth on God. His attitude was, "I represent the United States government, who is God compared to me?"

When that attitude came across, anger rose up inside of me. I stood up, poked my finger into his chest, and said, "Buddy, if God wants me to get drafted then I'll be drafted. And if He doesn't, you, nor the United States government, nor every demon in hell can't draft me." That might not have been the best way to handle it, but I was saying, I value God and His opinion more than what you have to say.

The recruiter never said another word. He looked at me, folded up all of his papers, put them in his briefcase, and walked out the door. I received my draft notice in the mail the very next morning! I didn't think about it back then, but I should have looked to see if it even had a postmark or stamp on it. I bet that guy went back to his office, processed my papers himself, and then put the draft notice in my mailbox!

I don't know if that's the way it happened and I didn't care, because I was trusting God. If I would have started valuing the recruiter's opinion over God's, I would have started the process of hardening my heart. Before long I would have felt like, "God, what happened to that experience where I knew how much You loved me and spoke to me, and changed my life?"

In hindsight, Vietnam was the best thing that ever happened to me. I was religious when I went to Vietnam. For the 13 months I was there, I studied the Word all day long. When I came back, I wasn't religious anymore. My theology had changed. I got hold of the grace of God and wasn't trying to fulfill religious duties to make myself worthy of God's love anymore. Vietnam was my Bible school; it was a good deal for me.

Magnify God, Not Your Problems

The flow of God's love can only be stopped by us. When we run into a dry spell, it isn't because God shut off the spigot. God speaks His love to us 24 hours a day, 7 days a week. One of the most common prayer requests I get is from people who want God to reveal His love to them. Their hearts are right in desiring to know God's love, but ignorance of God's love isn't the result of Him holding something back. God is constantly showering us with His love, so if we don't know the love of God it's because we aren't receiving what He has already given us. God loves us; no prayer is going to motivate God to love us more.

A woman once told me how she had been praying 20 years for her husband to be saved. She told me that God didn't answer her prayer but she believed He would answer mine. So she asked me to pray for God to save her husband. The way she phrased it made it sound like she thought it was up to God whether or not her husband received salvation. I told her, "God has already done everything about saving your husband He can do. He already sent His Son. He died. The Holy Spirit is working in you to help him get saved. You think that somehow or another God isn't motivated to save your husband, but He is more motivated for your husband to be saved than you are. You don't need to beg God to save your husband. Your husband needs to hear the Gospel and believe."

Faith comes by hearing and hearing by the Word of God. So I told her to pray for laborers to come across her husband's path to tell him about the Gospel. I told her to tell him the Good News herself, to love him, and to be a good example. Those are the things we can do to help someone get saved; we don't have to encourage God to save anybody. God is far more motivated about salvation than we are.

Sometimes when people receive the baptism of the Holy Spirit at one of my Gospel Truth Seminars, they have an ecstatic experience, get overwhelmed, and start speaking in tongues loudly, as if they can't control it. The baptism of the Holy Spirit is a good thing to get excited about, but I always stop them for a moment to show them that you don't have to feel ecstatic in order to pray in tongues. You won't always get goose bumps and have chills. It's great to feel those things, but you don't need to be emotionally overwhelmed to speak in tongues. You can pray in tongues whether you feel anything or not.

Someone might ask, "Are you saying that I can just turn the Holy Ghost on and off?" No, the Holy Ghost is *on* all of the time! People turn themselves on and off, but the Holy Spirit is always on. All you need to do is speak in tongues to turn yourself back on. The Bible tells us to build ourselves up in our holy faith by praying in the Holy Ghost, and to keep ourselves in the love of God (Jude 20-21). It's up to us whether or not we feel the love of God. It's up to us whether we are happy and joyful. It's not up to God.

God has placed His love, joy, and peace on the inside of us. Whenever we aren't feeling the love of God, it's because we have begun to value something else, diminishing what God has spoken to us. We can even lose our joy by esteeming our own efforts to please God instead of esteeming God's grace and the finished work of Jesus. So don't pray for God to give you joy again, just go back to valuing God and believing His Word.

Another word that means to glorify the Lord is *magnify*. The same Greek word that was translated "glorified" in Romans 1:21 was translated "magnify" in Romans 11:13. When we place value on God and focus on what He has done, it magnifies Him. Technically speaking, God is who He is, regardless of what we think. Ignoring God doesn't make Him smaller, just as failing to value or glorify God doesn't change how big He is, but it will change your perception.

You may not relate to God in a way that magnifies Him, but it's *your* value that gets altered, not His. The way we magnify God in our own lives is by placing value on Him and recognizing the things He is doing in our lives and the words He has spoken to us. Focusing on God makes Him get bigger in our way of thinking and perceiving. It makes Him bigger than sickness and tragedy. Magnifying God takes us to a place where we don't fall apart like a two-dollar suitcase every time something bad happens. Esteeming God above all circumstances will make Him big and everything else small. It not only changes our outlook; it changes our experience of life.

Our mind is like a set of binoculars: whatever we focus our attention on gets larger. It grows bigger and bigger and the more we think about it, the bigger it gets. The stuff that most people get upset about is insignificant relative to eternity. Most of the things people worry about won't make any difference a million years from now. In eternity we 'will all look back and think, "What was I so worried about?"'

Even though something is not a big deal; we often make it a big deal. If the devil puts a little toothpick in our path, we magnify it, focus on it, and think about it until it becomes a huge obstacle in our mind. Then we begin to believe the little splinter is a giant Redwood that we can't overcome, when in reality, the devil is just beating our brains out with a toothpick!

Sometimes, when people come to me with tears in their eyes and tell me what their problems are, I literally have to bite my lip to keep from laughing. I can't help thinking, I*s that all? This is what you're all upset over? I have worse things happen to me before I get out of bed in the morning.* But it's a big problem to them because they have magnified it. We need to do the exact opposite. We need to magnify God and focus on what He has done until our problems shrink in comparison.

There were eight or nine people with me in the prayer meeting that changed my life on March 23, 1968. Every one of us was impacted by God. We all knew that God had been in that room and we were all overwhelmed by His presence. My best friend was there so the next morning we talked about what had happened and we said we would never be the same.

Today, I am the only person who was in that room who still believes anything significant happened that night. Even though we all experienced the same thing, life, time, and adversity have talked them all out of the experience we shared. I'm the only one who still remembers what God did that night. As a matter of fact, my best friend who received the baptism of the Holy Spirit and spoke in tongues, renounces speaking in tongues today.

Another good friend of mine who was there that night went through some terrible times that forced him out of the ministry. He wound up having an affair and his life crashed. We parted ways a long time before any of that happened, but our friendship has been restored and I've asked him about some of the things we experienced together. I asked him if he remembered a time God spoke to us or when we witnessed a manifestation of God's presence or any of the other things we experienced that night. He didn't remember anything; he couldn't recall any of it.

The reason he couldn't remember the things God had done in his life was because he was very sensitive to people's opinions; he valued the opinions of men more than he valued God's opinion. He esteemed the approval of people above God, to the point that 42 years later, he couldn't even remember things that are as fresh to me as if they happened yesterday. This proves that whatever you focus on gets bigger, while everything else gets smaller by contrast. If you focus on the approval of people and the values of this world, the things of God will shrink in comparison. But if you magnify God, the opinions of people and your problems will shrink.

Very few days go by that I don't thank God for what He has done for me. I am constantly saying, "Thank You Father, for touching my life, and thank You for revealing Yourself to me." I glorify God and thank Him all the time. On the other hand, I have received a lot of criticism for preaching the Gospel. I have heard of people writing blogs against me on the Internet. Some of them claim that I am "the most dangerous man in America."

People say terrible things about me. I could get into self-pity and magnify the bad things that are being said, but I prefer to glorify the Lord, not my problems. I respond by saying, "Father, I don't know what their problem is but I know You love me. Thank You for touching my life." Because I have glorified God and put value on what He has done in my life, the events of March 23, 1968 are more powerful to me today than they were 42 years ago. I have never lost the joy of experiencing God's love for me.

God isn't responsible for turning off the flow of His power and love in our lives. Things can happen that make us lose sight of the truth—times of struggle wear us down and leave us feeling a lack of joy—but I have learned what to do when I start losing my joy. I immediately change my focus and begin to glorify God. As I do this, everything falls into proper perspective and my joy returns.

Problems happen in life. Businesses fail, people say hurtful things, and loved ones die, but magnifying those problems only makes them seem even more tragic than they really are, causing your esteem of God to shrink. In order to make God bigger in your mind than your problems, you need to change your focus.

Go back and remember the joy and peace you experienced when you were first saved. Begin to thank God for filling you with the Holy Spirit and placing the same power inside of you that raised Christ from the dead. Recall the times that God has touched you or healed you. As you glorify God and value what He has done in your life, all of the other incidents that have robbed your joy and peace will fade away. You don't have to ask God for a fresh touch. You can turn to Him and refresh yourself any time you want to be recharged.

I don't know if you listen to Christian music—or what is labeled as Christian music—but most of it is ungodly to the max. It's basically a Christian version of country and western music. Instead of complaining about losing your truck or your job, it whines about losing the presence of God. "*Oh God, touch me again, I'm desperate for You. I've lost your presence. Where did you go?*" Some of the songs I hear are pathetic. Not all Christian music, but a lot of it, is just whining, griping, and complaining to God. That's the reason I love Charlie and Jill LeBlanc's music. They sing lyrics like, "My favorite thing to do is to spend my time with You," and they glorify God instead of whining about what's going on. All whining does is verify, establish, and cement you into the problem you're in.

I admit that a lot of people go through mountain tops and valleys in their relationship with God, but it isn't because God wants it that way. You can keep yourself as happy as you want to be. If you aren't thrilled with God, it's not His fault. God hasn't failed you. You lose your joy when you quit glorifying God and start focusing on your problems. Magnifying your problems can be as subtle as telling someone all about your hurts and pains when they ask, "How are you?" Or it can be rehearsing in your mind the wrong someone has done to you; mulling over it again and again, until what was insignificant becomes a major concern.

I realize that not everyone wants to hear this. They say, "So you're saying my loss of joy and victory is my fault?" Yes, that's exactly what I'm saying—but don't get upset or feel condemned. This is great news because it means you can do something to change your experience. If God ordained us to go through mountaintops and valleys and only enjoy His presence for an hour before it wears off, then we would just have to deal with it. We can't do anything to change God. Discovering that the problem is with *us* is cause for celebration, because we can fix ourselves. We can change the way we think. We can do something about our behavior.

Stop focusing on your problems and begin to glorify God. Rehearse your victories and talk about how good God is. As you magnify God, all of your problems will shrink down to nothing. Sickness, disease, worry, hurt, grief, and pain will fade away as you focus on how good God is. Glorifying God and being thankful will keep you in God's will. It will keep you from getting discouraged and giving up.

In the 44 years that I have been seeking God, this principle has been one of the most important factors in keeping what God has done in my life fresh. I have never gotten over what God has done for me and I never will! I don't go a single day without thanking God for touching me and calling me into the ministry.

If I was God, I would have picked somebody more talented. I would have picked somebody better looking and who had a better voice. But I am so grateful that God chose me. I thank Him every day of my life for what He has done, therefore I'm as happy and excited about God as I was 42 years ago. Plus, now I have a lot more wisdom and experience. I wouldn't go back.

How many people, for one reason or another, talk about the "good ole' days?" I'm saying this with love, but if your days aren't good, it's your fault. This might be different from the way a lot of people think but that doesn't mean it's wrong. These principles are scriptural. I'm giving my testimony that glorifying God instead of my problems has changed my life. It's working for me and I've seen it work for others.

If the way you are living isn't producing the desired results, don't be resistant to change. If you are happy sometimes but depressed others, why hang onto the beliefs that are causing your up-and-down experiences? Focusing on God and valuing Him in my life has kept me from getting depressed, and I've had a lot of depressing things happen.

We take for granted the incredible reality that God has sent His Spirit to indwell us. We have received the same Holy Spirit that created the heavens and the earth. We have a lot to praise God for. We need to recognize that we are the ones who shut off the flow of God's love. God never turns off His supply; we turn it off when we esteem and glorify something other than Him. In order to stay on track and finish our course, we have to keep the things of God fresh in our lives. And the primary way to stay sensitive to God is to glorify Him above everything else.

Glorify the Lord

Chapter 14

Thankfulness Will Take You Places

Because that, when they knew God, they glorified Him not
as God, neither were thankful; but became vain in their
imaginations, and their foolish heart was darkened.

Romans 1:21

A s I pointed out in the last chapter, this scripture describes the steps that people take to deaden themselves to God. I'm turning these steps around to illustrate how we can stay sensitive to God and keep ourselves on track. Instead of failing to glorify God, being unthankful, and having a vain imagination, we want to glorify God, be thankful, and have a godly imagination. These few things will help keep us sensitive to God and fulfill our purpose.

We don't have to lose the joy in our relationship with God. In fact, our relationship with God should be getting better over time. Believers should be getting stronger and stronger in the Lord as time goes on. God never intended for the potency of our relationship with Him to fade, yet that is exactly what happens to the average Christian. God touched them at some point but the vibrancy of their experience faded. People tell me all the time how they had a powerful encounter with God at one of my Gospel Truth Seminars, but often they lose their excitement about the Lord once they get back home. It shouldn't be that way.

In the last chapter, I covered how the first step to staying sensitive to God and maintaining the intensity of our relationship is to glorify Him—to value His opinion above the opinions of men. But the factors listed here in Romans all work together; they are a package. For the purpose of discussion though, I separated them into different topics. This is really a description of a singular lifestyle on how to seek God and put Him first in your life. However, in terms of practical living, glorifying God, being thankful, and having a godly imagination aren't separate issues; they are all interconnected. So this second step of thankfulness is something we add to our lifestyle of glorifying God in all circumstances.

I will praise the name of God with a song, and will magnify him with thanksgiving.

Psalm 69:30

Jesus quoted several passages from this psalm when He was dying on the cross. This prophetic psalm was written by David hundreds of years before Jesus came to earth— but by the power of the Holy Spirit—this is Jesus speaking. He says that He will magnify God with thanksgiving. The way you make God look bigger than sickness, poverty, rejection, or any other problem is by thanking Him. Being thankful and rehearsing your victories makes God bigger in your perspective. It puts more glory, worth, and value on Him.

This is a powerful truth. Christians ought to be thankful people. We should rehearse our victories on a regular basis. In fact, this is the reason there are a number of scriptures in the Old Testament that commanded the Israelites not to take away their neighbor's landmark (Deuteronomy 19:14; 27:17; Proverbs 22:28; 23:10). Landmarks served as a reminder. For example, Samuel raised a stone and called it Ebenezer, which means "God is our help", because they won a great victory in battle (1 Samuel 7:12). Every time people passed by this landmark, it reminded them of the victory God won for them over the Amalekites. In the same way, we need to erect landmarks in our lives to remind us of the victories God has won for us.

One month before we taped the first show of our television program, I was working on a trail at my house and did something really stupid. I was trying to maneuver a huge boulder around and it ended up rolling over my head. I fell down and a 1,000 pound boulder rolled over my arm and bounced off my head. It should have killed me! The pain hit me immediately and I jumped straight up off the ground and ran a quarter of a mile screaming and praising God, before I even stopped to assess the damage. I wasn't sure my arm would still be there. God supernaturally protected me though, and the only damage I suffered was a swollen hand. (By the way, when I told Jamie that the boulder bounced off my head, she laughed and said, "Of course.")

As a memorial of what God did for me that day, I put a sign in front the boulder that says, "The Lord saved my life March the 23rd, 1999 when this boulder rolled over my head, arm, and hand." And then I wrote the scripture, "the Lord preserves the simple" (Ps 116:6). What I did was dumb. But God preserved me. Every time I walk by that boulder, the sign reminds me how God saved my life.

I erected another landmark on the face of a flat rock at the start of a trail on my property. It says, "If you don't, I will." It's a reference to when Jesus entered Jerusalem and He told the Pharisees that if the people didn't praise him, the rocks would immediately cry out (Luke 19:40). So every time I walk by that rock, I tell it to be quiet and I start praising God and thanking Him for all He has done in my life.

> *Bless the LORD, O my soul: and all that is within me, bless his holy name. Bless the LORD, O my soul, and forget not all his benefits.*
>
> *Psalm 103:1-2*

The reason this scripture tells us not to forget is because the natural human tendency is to focus on what's wrong and to forget what God has done for us. When 99 out of 100 things are going great in our lives, human nature will still focus on the one wrong thing. Our flesh tends to think that everything is falling apart even when all the evidence says that we are blessed. Carnal human nature will always focus on the negative. This is something I fight against and hate to see in myself, so I tend to be a little too hard on others when they come to me with small problems that they have blown out of proportion.

One Monday morning a long time ago, a student came into my office crying. He was somebody who always focused on his problems. He was crying so hard that it took me five minutes to calm him down enough so he could start telling me what the problem was. It turned out to be a silly issue. He was upset because when he was in church the day before, two women seated in front of him had talked and laughed throughout the entire service. He felt like the devil used those women to steal the Word from him. So I asked him, "Why didn't you move?" He never thought of that. He just sat through the entire service fuming with anger while binding and rebuking the devil.

Right before that student came into my office, I had just gotten off the phone with a friend of mine whose wife of 50 years died. I called him that morning to see how he was doing. He was praising God and thanking Him that he had been so happily married for 50 years! My friend was rejoicing and praising God in a circumstance that would have been a valid reason for sadness, while the student in my office was in tears because two people in front of him whispered during a church service.

I hate the natural tendency to get focused on the one little thing that is wrong in life. I don't like to see it in myself or in others. It will distort our perspective and keep us from seeing how blessed we truly are. When little problems come along, we have an inclination to magnify them until they take over our entire lives.

We can reverse this tendency by thanking God and focusing on the good.

A friend of mine, Pastor Bob, has a daughter who hit her head in a car accident a number of years ago. Not long after the accident, she started getting a few headaches and a couple of years later she had a seizure. She was rushed to the hospital but the doctors said she was brain dead. They didn't expect her to live through the day. She was on all sorts of life support equipment and it didn't look good.

Soon the doctor told Pastor Bob that his daughter was dead and it was time to take her off the life support equipment. He didn't get angry at what they said, he just told them that he was going to keep believing God. She has been under round the clock care in their home for more than a decade now. The doctors still say that she's brain dead, but she's making progress.

Dealing with the long-term illness of a loved one tends to wear on people. At one of our minister's conferences, Pastor Bob was sitting up front. I was preaching on how we magnify the negative and aren't appreciative for what we have and how we need to focus on the positive and glorify God. While I was talking, Pastor Bob stood up, threw his Bible on the floor and said, "I've had all of this I can take. I just have to thank God for how good things are." He started praising, shouting, and glorifying the Lord. When the people in the room who knew his situation saw how thankful he was, they started hitting their knees and asking God to forgive them for being focused on insignificant problems. Pastor Bob is one of the happiest guys I know. He is always looking to see if there is anything he can do for you. He lives his life for other people; you will never hear him complain.

In March 2000, Pastor Bob's church—an $18 million facility—was destroyed in 45 seconds when two tornadoes collided over it. A hundred people were in the building at the time and every single one of them was supernaturally protected. Within 30 minutes, CNN was broadcasting an interview with Pastor Bob. He was standing in front of the destroyed facility, wearing a hard hat and said, "God didn't do this. The devil did this. But we're going to come out of this better than before."

On the following Sunday, the local newspapers went to the auditorium in which his church was holding temporary services, expecting to continue their report on the devastation caused by the church's collapse. One reporter told them he was expecting to hear people cry and talk about what was lost, but instead the church members were acting as if they had won the lottery. People were running, jumping, and praising God because nobody was hurt during the tornadoes. They were also declaring how they were going to come out much better off than they were before this happened. Today, they have a facility twice as nice, plus a brand new building for their school with two gymnasiums and everything is paid for!

Whatever we focus on is what we magnify. We have to stop magnifying the negative. As Christians, we should magnify God with thanksgiving; we should be a thankful people. I don't believe we can use circumstances to discern what the will of God is, but if we look at Scriptural examples, we will notice that when things are tough it is a good indication that we're in the will of God. Just because we follow God doesn't mean that life is going to be all smooth sailing. Yet most people think that everything in life should be easy when they are serving God. I hate to break it to you but that isn't what the Lord promised us. Jesus said, "In the world ye shall have tribulation: but be of good cheer; I have overcome the world" (John 16:33).

God sent Paul and Silas into Macedonia, to the area of Philippi, and within days they were beaten and in stocks (Acts 16:19-23). But they didn't cry and whine about the situation they were in. At midnight they prayed and sang praises to God from their dungeon so all the prisoners could hear them. Suddenly, an earthquake shook the foundations of the prison, opened the doors, and broke open the prisoner"s chains. That's a pretty unusual earthquake (Acts 16:25-26).

Praise is powerful! The amazing thing is that Paul and Silas didn't even try to go anywhere after the earthquake freed them. They weren't praising God just to get free or to get something from Him. They were praising God because they loved Him. They were actually excited about God even while they were in a rat infested dungeon, their backs bleeding, facing possible execution.

A book entitled *Encyclopedia of Christian Martyrs* lists thousands of people who have been killed for their faith in Jesus. It tells about Christians during the Roman era who were so in love with the Lord that they would fight with each other to see who would get to go out and die for Jesus! Today, most people can't wrap their brain around such a desire.

One story tells of a woman who was eight months pregnant and awaiting execution in prison. All of her family and friends were going to be executed the next day in the Colosseum—by having wild beasts turned on them. However, the Romans wouldn't kill a pregnant woman, so her execution would have to wait until after she gave birth. She knew they would kill her as soon as her baby was born. She wanted to die in unity with her friends so she had her Christian brothers and sisters agree with her in prayer that the baby would be born early. She went into labor immediately and gave birth. A friend came to the prison to take her baby away and she went out the next day to be executed with her friends. They stripped off her clothing, put her in a net, and turned wild bulls loose that ripped her to pieces. The entire time she was glorifying God and thanking Jesus for the honor of dying in His name.

Not many people today focus on the goodness of God to that degree. We sing about what a great day it will be when we all get to heaven. But when the doctor tells us we are dying, we start to cry. Dying and going to be with Jesus isn't something most Christians are excited about today because most of us are more focused on the world than the things of God.

The Last Days

This know also, that in the last days perilous times shall come. For men shall be lovers of their own selves, covetous, boasters, proud, blasphemers, disobedient to parents, unthankful, unholy, without natural affection, trucebreakers, false accusers, incontinent, fierce, despisers of those that are good, traitors, heady, highminded, lovers of pleasures more than lovers of God.

2 Timothy 3:1–4

I don't know if you have figured this out or not, but we are living in the last days. The Apostle Peter said that the last days began over 2000 years ago on the Day of Pentecost (Acts 2:17), which puts us in the *last* of the last days. Scripture says that in the last days men will become lovers of themselves, and most people today are very self-centered. The very reason our lives are miserable is because we love ourselves so much. Self-love is like an addiction; you can't get enough of it. The more you get, the more you want. You can't satisfy self; self has to be denied. You need to get beyond thinking only of yourself. When you are all wrapped up in yourself, you make a very small package.

In the end times, it says, people will be covetous. Westerners are probably the most covetous people on the face of the earth. We have been taught to grab all we can, like a vacuum cleaner sucking up everything in its path. The American dream is to accumulate more and more. I'm not trying to make anyone feel condemned; I'm just pointing out the reality of where our society is today. Western society is very covetous. The Bible teaches us that covetousness is idolatry (Colossians 3:5). Most covetous people wouldn't say they are idol worshipers, but they are, and it's a sign of the end times.

In the last days, people will be boasters. I've seen this change come about in my own lifetime. At the core, people are the same as they have always been but they haven't always been so bold in their boasting. Back when I was young, people didn't go around announcing how awesome they were. It would have been considered pride and that kind of behavior was frowned upon. Nowadays, society seems to admire pride and boasting. People generally think it's a good thing to act like you're awesome and the world revolves around you. Sadly, even a lot of Christians act like that; they are boasters. They're proud. These negative traits are very descriptive of our world today.

Next, the scripture says men will become blasphemers. I've noticed that even the conservative talk show hosts on radio, who are supposed to be counter-culture to the liberal media, use profanity on a regular basis. Words that would have been considered completely unacceptable in conversation when I was a kid are used all of the time and people don't think anything about it. The scripture says children will be disobedient to parents. Is there anyone who doubts that children today are probably more disobedient to parents and more rebellious than ever?

The verse also says that in the last days people will be unthankful and unholy. Look at the list that being unthankful is included in. It's sandwiched right in there with people who lack natural affection and who are trucebreakers, false accusers, incontinent, fierce, despisers of those who are good, traitors, heady, high-minded, and lovers of pleasures more than lovers of God. Families are falling apart today because people don't have the natural love that should bind a family together; they are too selfish. The word *incontinent* in this verse means "having totally unrestrained emotions." People today are totally dominated and controlled by their emotions. Finally, the scripture says that people will be lovers of pleasure more than lovers of God. Without a doubt, people spend way more time and money on pleasure than they do on God.

Being unthankful is listed right in the midst of all these terrible traits that describe the end times we are living in. We are too focused on the negative. I'm telling you, if you want to finish your course and fulfill your destiny, one of the things you can do to keep your heart in the right place is to make the decision to bless the Lord at all times. You can get to a place where you are so positive that no matter what happens to you, you will find something to praise God about. Not that we won't have problems, but in the light of eternity, our problems are no big deal.

Eternal Perspective

For our light affliction, which is but for a moment, worketh for us a far more exceeding and eternal weight of glory; while we

*look not at the things which are seen, but at the things which
are not seen: for the things which are seen are temporal; but the
things which are not seen are eternal.*

2 Corinthians 4:17

Paul called his trials a "light affliction," yet he had a lot more problems than we do (2 Corinthians 11:23-27). He was beaten with rods three times. This punishment consisted of lifting a prisoner off the ground and beating the back of his calves, feet, and ankles with rods until the bones were broken. He said he was whipped so many times he couldn't count them all. He was imprisoned and persecuted more than any other person in Scripture. When I go to a city to preach the Gospel, I usually stay in a nice hotel. Paul, on the other hand, would end up in stocks in the lowest part of the dungeon. He endured tremendous persecution and rejection.

If Paul could call his persecution a light affliction, how can we believe our problems are such a heavy burden? It's because we don't have the same perspective that Paul had. As I said, our mind is like a pair of binoculars: whatever we focus on gets bigger. We can either magnify the little negative things or, by turning the binoculars around, we can look through the big end and even a huge mountain will shrink down to nothing. What we focus our attention on becomes bigger and what we neglect becomes smaller.

Paul was so focused on God that he could say, "For to me to live is Christ, and to die is gain" (Philippians 1:21). One of the ways we can get the same perspective is to remember that our afflictions are "but for a moment." Take any problem you might have right now and put it into the perspective of eternity. A thousand years from now, will whatever is bothering you still be a problem? Not even if your problems are life threatening! We are all going to die. You might live 40, 60, or 80 years, but we're all going to die unless Jesus comes back during our lifetime. We shouldn't be hanging on to this life like it's all we have. When we die, we go to be with the Lord. It's going to be awesome! The sufferings of this world are not even worthy to be compared with the glory that will be revealed when we go to be with Jesus (Romans 8:18).

I take care of my body by exercising and eating right because I believe I have a mission to complete, but if I was to die tomorrow it wouldn't bother me one bit. I'm making a difference through my life and ministry but I'm also excited about going to be with the Lord. It wouldn't bother me at all to check out. God would get somebody else to carry on what I'm doing. He would work it all out. Once you get that attitude, once you put things into an eternal perspective, the troubles you have in this life will shrink down to nothing in comparison.

I remember a woman who approached me for prayer one day after I finished preaching. She was crying as she told me that she was on her fourth marriage and her current husband wanted to divorce her. She couldn't stand the idea of getting divorced again so she tried to commit suicide the day before.

She said, "I'm not a Christian like you, but I know God is real and that prayer works. Would you please pray for me that I won't get divorced?"

"You're not a Christian," I asked, "and you know that you aren't a Christian?"

"Yes," she answered.

"And you want me to pray for your marriage, but you don't want to be born again?"

"That's right," she said.

I just looked at her for a moment.

"Don't you realize that after you've burned in hell for a thousand years, you won't give a rip whether your marriage worked or not?" I said, "Who cares about your marriage?"

She looked like I had just slapped her in the face.

She quit crying, looked at me, and said, "You know, I think you're right. I need to get saved."

"You sure do," I said. We prayed, she was born again, and *then* we prayed for her marriage.

I'm not saying God doesn't care about marriages. I'm saying that some people think that whatever hardship they are going through exempts them from the need to rejoice. It doesn't. Your salvation is more important than your marriage, health, or anything else. We aren't supposed to be happy about tragedy, but tragedy doesn't undo the goodness of God. Even when somebody dies, if they were a Christian, we can rejoice that they're in the presence of the Lord. It's normal to miss a person when they die, but the grief we feel is for us. There is no reason to feel sorry for somebody who has died and gone to be with the Lord. It doesn't matter if they died in an accident or prematurely; they are in the presence of God. It helps to understand that the grief we feel is for our own sense of loss. We need to recognize that the person is in heaven. It shrinks the loss down when you put it into the light of eternity.

Having an eternal perspective will change your way of thinking about everything. If the doctor tells you that you are going to die, it won't be a big deal. We know that God wants us well (3 John 1:2) and it's His will to heal everyone, but the worst-case scenario is that we go to be with the Lord (2 Corinthian 5:8). Having an eternal perspective rids us of fear, stress, and worry. The Bible says that a merry heart does good like a medicine (Proverbs 17:22). You could thank God that you're in a win-win situation: when you get healed, you can travel the world telling people how God healed you; but if for some reason you don't get healed, then you get to go be with the Lord. You can't lose for winning. As you start being thankful and magnifying God, your immune system will work better and you will probably see your healing manifest. You win by becoming a thankful person. Start by thanking God every morning just for being alive.

Everything you can see is temporary: your house, car, clothes, everything. But the things you can't see are eternal. Paul wasn't just looking at the natural realm. He wasn't focused on his house, assets, or retirement. He was looking at intangible, eternal things. That's how you fulfill God's will for your life.

Jesus is the same yesterday, today, and forever (Hebrews 13:8). If your focus and value is on the Lord, you won't fluctuate with circumstances. Joy that comes and goes is a sign that you aren't focused on God. You don't have to live like an unbeliever, just trying to satisfy your carnal desires. You can live to glorify God. You can thank God every day. Maybe events in your life aren't perfect, but you can always find something to praise God for.

Being thankful is how we fight against the natural human tendency to focus on problems. Actually, being thankful and glorifying God are very closely related. We can't truly glorify God unless we are thankful. Our carnal nature tends toward forgetting the goodness of God. One of the things we must do to stay thankful is rehearse our victories and remember the good things that God has done for us. Problems are going to come, but having an eternal perspective will give us the momentum to roll right over trouble.

If we are traveling at 1,000 miles per hour, the devil can put a brick wall in our path and it won't stop us. In the same way, we can build up so much momentum in our Christian life that no problem can take away our joy or keep us from glorifying God. To fulfill God's will, we are going to have to develop this attitude. We need to glorify God and keep our hearts sensitive to Him by being thankful; then we will see that life works much better.

Chapter 15

Putting Your Imagination to Work

Because that, when they knew God, they glorified him not as God, neither were thankful; but became vain in their imaginations, and their foolish heart was darkened.

Romans 1:21

The passage we have been studying reveals that the last step in hardening your heart toward God is becoming vain in your imagination. Again, the steps we have been discussing are not disconnected. Knowing God but failing to glorify Him, being unthankful, and having a vain imagination are sequential steps in the process of walking away from the Lord. The first thing that happens is you let something other than God occupy your attention and start valuing the opinions of others above God. After you stop glorifying God, you become unthankful and finally your imagination becomes vain, which doesn't mean it stops working, it means it starts working against you. It might mean you start imagining failure instead of success. One thing leads to another and the end result is a hardened heart.

Adults often wrongly believe that using their imagination is the same as fantasizing, but it isn't. *Imagination* is defined as "the act or power of forming a mental image of something not present to the senses or never before wholly perceived in reality."[3] For example, you probably haven't counted how many doors are in your house. But if I asked you how many doors are in your house, you could bring up a mental image of your house and count the doors by going through the picture in your mind. You aren't seeing the space with your physical eyes; you are using your imagination. We do the same thing when someone asks us for directions and we visualize the route in our mind as we give instructions. Imagination is the ability to see something with your mind, or your heart, that you can't see with your eyes.

We can't function in our daily life without using our imagination. We think in pictures. When the word "apple" is spoken, we don't envision the letters a-p-p-l-e, we see a mental image of an apple. Some people might see a green apple, while others see a red apple, but the word "apple" still brings an image to our mind. We can't really understand something until we can picture it in our mind, which is why people say a picture is worth a thousand words. If we can picture something, we can do it!

In Vietnam, we got our water from water blivetts. Most of you can't picture a water blivett, therefore you won't be able to remember this or describe it to others. Water blivetts are black cylinder-looking rubber containers with brass ends. They were

---

[3] Definition of "imagination." In Merriam-Webster dictionary online, accessed February 22, 2013 http://www.merriam-webster.com

flown into us by helicopters in 250, 500 and 1,000 gallons sizes. Each had a spigot on the end we used to fill our water containers. As the water came out, the atmospheric pressure would collapse the blivett and it would become flat. Then the helicopter would pick the empty blivett up and carry it away.

You still may not have a great picture in your mind of a water blivett, but the words I used to describe it painted a picture in your imagination, so now you have some concept of what a water blivett is. You will be able to remember what it is because you have an image to attach to it.

This is why architects use blueprints: to show the builders how to construct what they have imagined. Our ministry is in the process of designing buildings for construction at our new campus in Woodland Park, Colorado. We sat together for hours talking about how we want the auditorium to look. It's a process of forming a mental image. Once we were able to picture in our imaginations what we want, the architects can build it.

Imagination is further defined as creative ability and resourcefulness.[4] You can't create without an imagination. Not long ago, I built a deck at my house. I'm not an experienced builder; I just wanted the challenge of building something so I constructed a three level deck. While I was planning, I used to sit on a bucket and imagine what I wanted the deck to look like. I didn't have a blueprint or anything. I just pictured it in my mind. After I was able to imagine it on the inside, I was able to build it.

---

[4] Ibid.

Imagination isn't just for little kids. You can't function without it. Imagination helps us understand abstract concepts like mathematics. Some people struggle with comprehending math, but a good teacher will illustrate math problems in a way that helps students understand. Instead of saying "two plus two equals four," they will draw a word picture. For example, "If you have two pieces of apple pie on your plate and you add two pieces of peach pie, how many pieces of pie are on your plate?" People will begin to see the relevance if you can get them to picture the concept in their minds. A good teacher is someone who paints pictures with words and helps the listener visualize ideas.

You can't see anything happen without your imagination. If you can't see something on the inside, you won't be able to see it manifest in your life. If you can't see yourself healed or 'imagine yourself healthy, you won't see healing manifest in your body. A lot of people know that God can heal, but in their imagination they see themselves as a sick person. They see themselves suffering and in pain. Some people have been sick for so long that they even see themselves being sick in their dreams. Their imagination is still working, but it's working against them; it has become vain.

Memory is also tied to imagination, from simple things like remembering where we parked our car to recalling the neighborhood we grew up in. Most people don't write down where they parked their car when they go somewhere. They don't remember specific instructions like take a left turn after the lamp post, walk ten steps and turn right, bear left, etc. They just have a mental image of where they left their car. In the same way, we have a mental image of where we grew up.

Sometimes, the image we have is different from reality. I grew up not too far from a patch of woods that I used to play in as a little kid. I remember riding my bike into the cool darkness during summer and having to wait while my eyes adjusted. It was a special place to me. As an adult, I recalled that space being miles and miles wide, but when I went back and saw it later in life, it was just one small acre of trees. The woods had grown in my memory over time because images inside of us can be affected or polluted by a lot of different factors.

The word *imagination* and variations of *imagine,* are used 36 times in the Bible. One of the words translated as "imagination" is the Hebrew word *yetser.* Yetser is also translated "mind" in the scripture, "Thou wilt keep him in perfect peace, whose mind is stayed on thee: because he trusteth in thee" (Isaiah 26:3). When the verse tells you to keep your mind stayed on the Lord, it's talking about more than just having thoughts concerning God. It means think about God until an image is painted on the inside of you and you begin to see things from His perspective. This is why many people don't understand the power that's in the Word of God. They only look on the surface level. They may get a glimpse of something but they don't meditate on it until they see it clearly on the inside.

Imagination is a very important concept to understand; it is one of the things that will allow us to fulfill God's will. Believers can't live on a surface-level understanding of the things of God. We have to go beyond the surface, to the point, where the Word of God literally changes the way we see things with our heart.

I heard a story about a pastor's wife who was almost blind. Her glasses were so thick that they looked like the bottom of a soda bottle. A healing evangelist was preaching at their church one day, so she was trying to avoid him. Many people had prayed for her eyes in the past, but her eyes had never been healed and she didn't want to go through that whole experience again. But the healing evangelist cornered her at one of the services.

"I want to pray for you," he said.

He made her take her glasses off and commanded her eyes to be healed. When he was done he asked, "Can you see?"

The woman started to open her eyes to check her vision, but the healing evangelist stopped her.

"Shut your eyes!" he ordered.

She shut her eyes quickly.

"Can you see?" he asked.

As soon as she started to open her eyes, he commanded again, "Shut your eyes!"

They repeated the same exchange a third time. Confused, she was standing there with her eyes closed wondering, "What is this man doing? How can I tell if I can see if I don't open my eyes?"

Then she heard the evangelist say, "I didn't tell you to open your eyes. You have to see yourself seeing on the inside before you can see on the outside."

She stood there with her eyes closed thinking about what he said. Within a few minutes she understood what he was asking her. He was asking, "Can you see yourself seeing? In your imagination, are you blind or can you see?"

She prayed in tongues for a while and finally said, "I can see myself seeing."

"Now, open your eyes," he told her.

When she opened her eyes, her vision was perfect.

Conception

A lot of people miss what God has for them because even though they ask for healing, they see themselves sick. They have been sick for so long that the sickness is not just in their body, the sickness has spread to their mind and emotions. When they pray, they are hoping something will happen but they don't really believe on the inside that it will. They don't see themselves well on the inside. Their imagination has become vain and is working against them: they see themselves sick and they don't really believe anything is going to change.

Now faith is the substance of things hoped for, the evidence of things not seen.

Hebrews 11:1

Hope is your imagination (Romans 8:24-25) and faith is the substance of things hoped for. If you can't hope for something first (imagine it) then you can't receive it by faith. A lot of people try to believe they are healed but they have never started *hoping* they are healed. They don't have the image that they are healed on the inside, so their faith has nothing to motivate it and keep it on track.

One of the things you need to have when it comes to fulfilling God's will and staying consistent over a long period of time, is a strong sense of hope. Hope is the anchor of your soul (Hebrews 6:19). An anchor is what keeps a ship from being blown around. Hope will keep you from being blown off course and missing your destination. You need a vision—an image on the inside of you. Until you can see it on the inside, you won't see it on the outside.

A person who has seen a loved one die from sickness or mental disease can get an image of that illness burned into their mind. They can start to believe that illness runs in the family. It might not be a conscious thought, but they can see themselves dying from the same illness. They half expect it to happen so it becomes a self-fulfilling prophecy, because whatever image you have of yourself will eventually bear fruit (Proverbs 23:7).

You need to see yourself as God sees you. His vision is revealed in the Word of God. Moses was 120 years old when he died and yet his eyesight was not dim nor his natural force abated (Deuteronomy 34:7). In our society, people talk about being "over the hill" at 40. They look at sick people in their 70s or 80s and think,

"I'm going to be like that one day." People start talking about and anticipating the problems they are going to have and it becomes a self-fulfilling prophecy. You have a superior covenant to what Moses had, so if he could live 120 years and be healthy, you can too. You have to change the way you think. Study the Word and imagine the truths of God until it paints a picture on the inside of you, until you see yourself healthy, righteous, and full of peace and joy.

The Hebrew word *yetser* that is translated "imagination" also means "conception"."This reveals a significant truth: your imagination is where you conceive things. This is really important. When a couple wants to have a baby, they can't just pray for one—they have to conceive the child. I have prayed for a lot of couples who were having trouble conceiving a baby. After I prayed for them to be healed I always said, "This isn't going to be a virgin birth. You have a part to play in this situation. Faith without works is dead, so go and do your part." A baby has to be conceived through a physical relationship, you can't just pray for one. Similarly, your imagination is where you conceive a manifestation of God's miracle-working power. No imagination equals no conception.

Many people don't meditate on the Word of God until they conceive something. They throw out a prayer like, "Oh, God, heal me," or "Supply this need," but they haven't ever conceived from the Word what they are asking for. It's the equivalent of a married couple praying that a stork will bring them a baby. It isn't going to happen that way. First, you have to conceive what the Word says in your imagination. For example, you have to see yourself healed.

The building that our ministry is currently in is 110,000 square feet, but when we bought the building only 10,000 square feet was finished office space. The rest was an empty warehouse. After the architects drew up the plans and we were waiting for the funding to start on the construction, I had them place tape on the floor where all of the walls would be.

I spent hundreds of hours walking around inside the taped lines in that empty warehouse. I was *seeing* the walls in place and *picturing* how everything was going to look. I never stepped over the tape; I always entered where a door would be. Some people might think this is strange, but I was helping my imagination. I would look at the architect's drawings and then walk around inside the taped lines, imagining all the walls in place. I would see people inside the auditorium. In fact, I put a piece of plywood on top of several five gallon buckets and stood on the platform and preached. No one was even in the building; it was nighttime and the warehouse was dark, but I preached like the auditorium was filled to capacity.

I used my imagination to see what I was believing God to do. On the day we held the dedication ceremony after the building was completed, everyone was excited to see what God had done. A woman came up to me and said, "You don't look very excited. Aren't you delighted to have the building complete?" I was excited, but it was almost anti-climactic to see it with my eyes because I had already seen it in my heart. For more than a year, I had seen on the inside what just then became visible to the physical eye. By the time construction was completed, I was ready to move on to the next task God had for me.

Today, very few visionaries exist because life tries to beat this attitude out of us. Most kids are told by the adults around them to quit dreaming, to quit using their imagination. Adults tend to think of visualizing the future as fantasizing, but there is a big difference between imagination and fantasy. Imagination is the power, or process, of seeing something that you can't see with your physical eyes, whereas fantasy is delusion. Fantasy is imagining something that isn't real; it's fiction. I'm not talking about day-dreaming. I'm talking about knowing the Word of God and seeing the spiritual truths it reveals. A sanctified, godly imagination is the part of you that conceives the things of God; it's the creative part of you that has a vision for the future.

Vision, in this sense, isn't seeing with your eyes; it's seeing with your heart. As a born-again believer filled with the Holy Spirit, you have the ability to see things that can't be seen with the natural eye. When I pray for people, I see them healed in my imagination. I see God touching their hearts. God will show me parts of a person's body that are injured or sick. I don't see it with my eyes; I get a mental picture.

Take the Word of God and let it soak down into the creative part of your mind—your imagination—until you can see yourself successful or healed. Allow the Word to get down inside of you and generate vision, until you see yourself laying hands on the sick and watching them recover or see the business you want to start successful.

A godly imagination is directly tied to glorifying God and being thankful. The Bible says that if you don't glorify God and if you aren't thankful, your imagination becomes vain (Romans 1:21). It's automatic. Instead of being creative and conceiving good things, a vain imagination conceives evil.

Some children are told from a young age that they aren't wanted or that they will never amount to anything. Other people in society are put down because of their skin color, lack of education, or socioeconomic status. When we believe the negative words or ideas that are pushed on us, it forms an image on the inside of us about who we are and what we can do. That image becomes a ceiling we can't rise above. Even though our talents and abilities could enable us to go further, we 'don't allow them to. Somehow we find a way to self-destruct.

I have a very good friend whose father was pretty hard on him as a kid. They had a lot of cars on their property and his father would make him help work on the cars. He told him, "You're so stupid, you can't screw a nut on a bolt without crossing the threads." Over the years, I have worked with my friend on a number of cars and it seems like every time he puts a nut on a bolt, he cross threads it. He would put it on once and it would be okay, but then he would say, "I think I've cross threaded it." So he would take the nut off and put it back on five or six times, trying to get it right. Eventually, he would cross thread the bolt. He had a negative image painted on the inside of him that still affects him.

A lot of us have been cursed in this way. You might not call it being "cursed," but that's what it is. Maybe you were cursed or you cursed yourself by being self-critical, or maybe you have done some really stupid things that have caused you to see yourself as a failure. All of these things will cause your imagination to become vain. You don't see yourself being who God says you are. God says you can lay hands on the sick and they shall recover (Mark 16:18), but you don't see it. You see yourself as a "nobody," and religion reinforces the idea that you are an unworthy nobody. It teaches you to think, "Who am I to think God wants to do anything for me?" Then the experiences of life come along to strengthen all the negative images you have formed about yourself.

Glorifying God, putting value and worth on Him and being thankful will cause your imagination to come alive and start working for you. Instead of conceiving negative images, you'll start to conceive positive ideas. A positive imagination will help erase all of the self-defeating ideas you have wrongly believed about yourself and you will begin to imagine yourself the way God sees you.

I had a chance to visit with Oral Roberts in 2009 and it made my imagination come alive. I don't agree with everything Oral Roberts did, but he had a heart for God and I can learn from him. You can't be so biased that you won't listen to anyone who doesn't agree with you 100%. Here's a news flash: *you don't have it all together either.* Nobody does. But we can still learn from one another. It's the same as if you are driving down the interstate and someone is five hours down the road in front of you. It doesn't matter if they are the greatest person or have made all of the right decisions, they can still tell you what the road is like, where you can eat, or where to buy gas.

I learned things from Oral. Hearing him tell about the things God had spoken to him inspired my imagination. Within a matter of months of speaking with Oral, God led me into the next major step for our ministry. Being around people who talk about vision causes you to dream big also. Most people think too small. They aim at nothing and hit it every time. It has become a cliché, but you need to aim for the stars; even if you miss, you might hit the moon.

When we were constructing the Charis Bible College facility in Colorado Springs, Colorado, we tried to get it finished by August so we could start the school year in the new building. It wasn't finished until November though, so it put us in a little bit of a bind. The old building was just way too small. One of the inconveniences was that we didn't have enough toilets, so the men had to use portable outdoor toilets, and Colorado gets cold in October. When we finally moved into the new building, I had somebody ask me if it was a disappointment not to make the move by August. I said, "We raised 3.2 million dollars above our normal expenses in fourteen months. I'd call that a smashing success." Being three months late was no big deal. I've never done anything perfectly in my life, so it didn't bother me. I still had a great miracle come in. We have to focus on the positive.

In order for your imagination to function positively, you need to spend time being quiet and still. Being busy with the things of this world and constantly watching television or listening to the radio will choke out your imagination. You have to spend some time being quiet and letting your imagination run wild. Be still and know that God is the Almighty. You might be amazed what things you conceive, and once you see it on the inside, you will see it on the outside.

Understanding

In the New Testament, the same word that is translated "imagination" is sometimes translated "understanding." The Bible is full of references to the importance of having understanding. In the Gospel of Matthew, Jesus taught that when people lack understanding, Satan will come and steal the Word that has been sown in their hearts (Matthew 13:19). Understanding is how we get something down on the inside of us. We have to let the truths of God go beyond mental awareness and down to the level of understanding until we can conceive a picture in our imagination.

Understanding is more than just knowledge or the ability to recall a fact. A lot of people read the Bible with their head, not with their imagination or heart. That's like chewing food but not swallowing it. The Word won't minister to us at its fullest until we get it down to the level of understanding. It isn't enough to merely hear the things of God. We have to meditate on the Word until it paints a picture, until we truly see what is happening. That's how we use our imagination to conceive the things of God in our heart.

I remember reading about David and Goliath when I was a kid. Scholars believed Goliath was nine feet nine inches tall, so I went outside and marked that height on a tree. Then I bent over until I was about five feet tall, which is how tall they thought David was. I wanted to get an image of what David was facing. You don't necessarily need to act out Bible stories, but you will get more out of the Word of God once you engage your imagination.

Eventually, I traveled to Israel on a tour. On a particularly hot day, we were on a bus that passed through the valley of Elah where David fought Goliath. They asked if anybody wanted to get off the bus. It was so hot that I was the only one who wanted to leave the air conditioning. I got off the bus and walked down to a little streambed that ran through the valley. I picked up five small stones and stood there wondering what it must have been like for David to face Goliath with five little rocks. The reason people say that visiting Israel makes the Bible more real to them is because being "on-location" engages their imagination. Once they see it, the Word comes alive.

Very few people meditate on the Word. Most simply read it in order to check off another good work on their list of religious duties, hoping it will obligate God to move in their lives. They read the Bible out of compulsion so they run through it as fast as they can. After all, we wouldn't want to miss our favorite television show. At that level, we are just reading words and putting information in our brain. It never makes its way down into our heart or imagination, so we never conceive anything. It doesn't become alive to us.

Imagination isn't something we can afford to ignore. I've heard of a multi-millionaire entrepreneur who travels and speaks about business and wealth. Every week, he takes one day off just to be quiet and think. He 'doesn't conduct any business on that day; he just takes inventory of where he is and where he is going. Essentially, he is fueling his imagination. This is one of the practices that helped him succeed and earn millions of dollars.

We would be much better off if we spent time encouraging our imaginations. We can't allow other people to spoon feed us all the time. We also have to ask God what He has for us. We can't let what other people have said determine our identity and future. We need to find out what the Word says about us. Then we need to pray and let the Holy Spirit give us an image of what He wants us to do and who He wants us to be. We can't become who God says we are until we can see ourselves as He sees us. Once we can see it on the inside, we can become it on the outside.

We will become exactly what we imagine, whether that image is positive or negative. If we think we are a failure, we will be. We have to deal with our imagination and get it to line up with God's opinion of us.

Greater Things

I began believing it was possible to see people raised from the dead after reading what Jesus said in the Gospel of John:

Verily, verily, I say unto you, He that believeth on me, the works that I do shall he do also; and greater works than these shall he do; because I go unto my Father.

John 14:12

I read that verse and it inspired me to believe that God would do miracles through me. I thought about all of the miracles Jesus performed. I meditated on how Jesus called Lazarus out of his tomb, and asked, "Father, can I raise someone from the dead?" I meditated on it so much that I raised a dozen people from the dead every night in my dreams. I had dreams about going into morgues and emptying them out. After about six months, I actually saw a person raised from the dead with my physical eyes, but I had to see it with my heart first.

How you see yourself is important. You have to see yourself as able to do, or be, the things you are praying for. You won't see miracles come to pass if you don't believe that God can do a miracle through you. It needs to become so real in your imagination that you dream about it.

I saw two people raised from the dead, but then ten or fifteen years went by before I saw it again. One day, I remembered how I used to meditate on seeing people raised from the dead and decided that I needed to get my imagination going again in that area. I felt inspired by God to start imagining people being raised from the dead, so pretty soon I was dreaming about it.

Then, one night, I got a phone call that my own son had died. He had been dead for four and a half hours when I got the phone call. But I just started thanking God for His goodness and magnifying Him above the circumstances. By the time I arrived at the hospital, my son had come back to life. It wouldn't have happened if I hadn't been meditating and imagining God's "raising-from-the-dead" power.

Before you see something happen, you have to be focused on it. It has to become so real that you see yourself doing it in your dreams. You won't see the miracle power of God if you are defeated, discouraged, or depressed in your imagination. The Word says, as a man thinks in his heart so is he (Proverbs 23:7). You have to resurrect your imagination and start using it in a positive way.

Hope

I researched every time the word *imagination* was used in the Bible and with the exception of one verse (1 Chronicles 29:18), it was always used in a negative way. For instance, God saw that the imagination of men's hearts was only evil continually (Genesis 6:5). At the tower of Babel, God said that nothing men could imagine would be restrained from them, so He divided language so men wouldn't be united anymore (Genesis 11:6-7). (It's worth noting that God recognized that the cumulative imagination of men could threaten His purpose for mankind. This shows how powerful imagination is.)

In the New Testament, it says, "For the weapons of our warfare are not carnal, but mighty through God to the pulling down of strong holds; casting down imaginations, and every high thing that exalteth itself against the knowledge of God, and bringing into captivity every thought to the obedience of Christ" (2 Corinthians 10:4-5). Imagination is always referred to as negative. It used to puzzle me that imagination could be such a powerful thing, but always carry negative connotations in Scripture. I prayed about it until the Lord showed me the answer:

> *For we are saved by hope: but hope that is seen is not hope: for what a man seeth, why doth he yet hope for? But if we hope for that we see not, then do we with patience wait for it.*

Romans 8:24-25

Hope, according to Scripture, is seeing something that you can't physically see. It's no longer hope if you can see it. Hope is seeing something with your heart that you can't see with your eyes—which is exactly what imagination is. It's the ability to see something that isn't present; the ability to see with your heart. I believe that hope is the scriptural word for a positive imagination. Hope is your imagination working for you, instead of against you.

We need a strong sense of hope. "Faith is the substance of things hoped for, the evidence of things not seen" (Hebrews 11:1). Faith only provides what hope has already seen. Hope is to faith, what a thermostat is to an air conditioning system. Hope turns on the ability of God while faith is the power that makes things come to pass.

I heard Charles Capps tell a story about a thermostat one time. It was probably made up, but the story illustrates a good point. He told about a man from the mountains who had never been around modern conveniences. He went to a meeting in the city. The meeting room he was in became hot as it filled with hundreds of people. The man was fanning himself to cool down, as he watched an usher walk by him and turn a dial on a small box that was mounted on the wall. Shortly thereafter, he started to feel cool air blowing on him. He was overwhelmed, so he went and asked the usher what he did to make the air cold.

"What do you mean?" the usher asked.

"You turned that little thing on the wall and cold air started blowing," the man said.

"Well, yeah, it's a thermostat," the usher answered.

"Can I get one of those?" the man asked.

"Of course you can," he answered, "they sell them at any hardware store."

The man was excited and went straight to the hardware store to buy one. When he got back to his cabin in the mountains, he mounted the thermostat on the wall. He turned the dial and sat down to wait for the cold air. But, of course, nothing happened because the thermostat has to be connected to an air conditioning system. A thermostat doesn't cool air; it activates the power unit which cools the air.

Likewise faith only produces what hope has already seen. You have to have hope—or a positive imagination in your heart—that sees miracles happening. Just like a thermostat can be turned to hot or cold, your imagination can be negative or positive. Hope is a positive imagination. If your imagination is negative, you will see failure on the inside, leading you to experience failure on the outside. But if you are hoping and seeing a miracle in your heart, it will turn on the power of God to see that miracle manifest in your life.

Faith will either work *for* you or *against* you. A negative image will cause everything in you to work toward making the negative image you have bear fruit. You have to change the image that is inside of you by creating hope. Hope comes through the Word of God (Romans 15:4). This is the first step of faith.

Notice that the scripture says we are saved by hope, because we wait with patience for what we do not see. Earlier, I taught how important patience is in fulfilling God's will for our lives. I also shared that patience is simply faith over a prolonged period of time. Patience is also linked to hope and your imagination. If you have a strong sense of hope or a strong imagination, then you will have the patience to wait for God's will to manifest in your life, even if it takes a long time.

A strong sense of hope will cause you to know beyond the shadow of a doubt that God's will is going to come to pass. You will know it in your heart and expect it, because your imagination has made it real. No matter what might be going on in your life, you will know that you have what you are waiting for.

Our *Healing Journeys II* DVD tells the story of a woman named Merci Santos, who was healed of multiple sclerosis. One of the things she said was when she was in a wheelchair and everyone told her that she would never walk again, she just knew it wasn't true. She saw herself healed and knew that one day she would be. She needed someone to teach her some things and activate her faith, but she saw herself well despite the fact that her symptoms were getting worse and worse. That is what hope is. Hope won't get you healed, but it will provide the motivation for your faith to get you healed.

Sometimes, you just need to be real with yourself and say, "I may not be in a place right now where I can really believe that I'm going to be healed instantly, but I'm in the process of hoping. I'm building my hope and I'm beginning to paint an image on the inside that I will be healed."

I met a man who had been diagnosed with bone cancer. He believed that he would be healed, and he was, but during the process doctors surgically removed a part of his pubic bone. He wanted to use his faith to believe that his pubic bone would grow back. That's pretty strong faith, to grow something back that was cut out. Anyway, he cut out pictures of a human skeleton from an encyclopedia and put the pictures up in his house. He started to imagine his pubic bone growing back and in a short period of time it did. *He saw it on the inside and it came to pass on the outside!*

We are living at such a substandard level in comparison with what God intends for us. Most of us don't have a clue about the extent of the power that God has placed inside of every born-again believer. I can show you scriptures that say we have the same power inside of us that raised Christ from the dead. But it doesn't matter whether you can quote Scripture, you have to believe it.

Can you see yourself raising the dead? Have you seen yourself standing against the devil and overcoming illness or poverty? Can you see yourself doing the miracles Jesus did? We have to meditate on the Word of God until we can see ourselves doing these things. We have to get our imagination working. The reason the Word says that hope is so powerful is because once you can see a manifestation of God's power with your heart, you can see it materialize in your life.

The Heart

A positive imagination is a byproduct of being truly thankful and valuing the things of God (Romans 1:21). Prizing God and being thankful will cause your imagination to come alive, and you will start seeing things differently than you have ever seen them before. But if you don't magnify God and remain thankful, your imagination will become negative and then your heart becomes hardened. The scripture we have been studying says that they "became vain in their imaginations, and their foolish heart was darkened" (Romans 1:21). A foolish, darkened heart is a hardened heart and once your heart is hardened, you are separated from the life of God (Ephesians 4:18).

It's tragic, but most people live somewhere between a vain, negative imagination and a hardened heart. They only imagine bad things, so when the doctor tells them they are going to die, they start planning their funeral. They see themselves dying and start to imagine what is going to happen when they are gone. Such a vain, negative imagination works against them and causes a hardened heart. Having a hard heart doesn't necessarily mean you aren't trying to love God or follow His will for your life; it means that you don't understand how much God loves you totally separate from your behavior or performance.

People with hardened hearts only see and understand the Word of God with their brain. Moving beyond that stage takes time and effort. You have to start obeying God, meditating on the Word, glorifying the Lord, and being thankful. As you focus more on God, your imagination will come alive and you will have a strong sense of hope about your future and the things God has promised you. Those practices will keep you focused on God and what He has already done for you, instead of being focused on yourself. It will help you stay on track to fulfill God's will for your life.

You need to have a vision that you are moving toward. Vision is nothing but hope for the future or a positive imagination. Vision will give you the motivation to keep going and the focus to fulfill God's will for your life. The Apostle Paul wrote,

> *While we look not at the things which are seen, but at the things which are not seen: for the things which are seen are temporal; but the things which are not seen are eternal.*

> *2 Corinthians 4:18*

How was Paul looking at things that can't be seen? He was seeing them with his heart or imagination. I was at a Charis Bible College meeting in Colorado one time when my wife was singing "Hallelujah" and everyone was worshipping God. The presence of the Lord was powerful. I was standing there with my eyes closed, and all of a sudden, I saw a picture in my mind of Jesus walking in through a set of double doors to my left. He walked through the doors and stood there as the doors slowly closed behind Him. He stood there for a moment looking around. Then he walked up to a woman on the front row and touched her; she fell to the floor, worshipping and praising God. Then He walked past two people and touched another woman. When Jesus touched her, she went down on her knees, lifted up her hands, and started worshipping God. My eyes were closed the whole time; I was seeing this happen in my imagination.

What I was seeing in my imagination was so real that I opened my physical eyes to see if it was really happening. When I opened my eyes, the two doors on my left flew open. I couldn't see anyone standing there, but the doors burst open and then slowly closed. Just after the doors closed, the woman I had seen Jesus touch in my imagination fell flat on the floor. A moment later, the second woman hit her knees and started praising God. Everything I saw in my imagination happened. I saw it with my physical eyes, except I couldn't see Jesus. All I could see with my eyes were the physical things that were happening. I couldn't see what was happening in the spiritual realm.

I could actually see better with my heart than I could with my eyes, so I closed my eyes again. In my imagination, I saw Jesus stand beside me and minister to me. Then I saw Him walk down the center aisle of the room and touch some other people. I kept my eyes closed and watched it all play out in my imagination. I could see it better on the inside than I could see it with my physical eyes. After the service was over, I went up to the people I saw Jesus touch in my imagination and asked them if they experienced anything during the service. They told me what had happened to them and it was exactly what I had seen in my heart.

God created us to be so much more than most of us are experiencing. Most of us are going through this life half blind, only seeing with our natural eyes. If you try to run a race half blind, you are probably going to trip over something. Likewise, you can't fulfill God's will for your life without using your heart to see.

Getting into the presence of God will allow you to see things in your imagination. Everything in the physical might be indicating one thing, but in your heart the Word of God can paint a picture of something else. The natural evidence might suggest that your business is going to fail, but you can have an image on the inside and know beyond the shadow of a doubt that it will succeed. Conceive the miracle in your imagination, then watch it come to pass.

No one is more blind than a group of people who direct their lives by what they can only physically see, sense, or understand. Faith is the ability to see things that aren't physically present. You must have a vision to fulfill God's will for your life. Proverbs says that where there is no vision, the people perish (Proverbs 29:18). Many people are falling by the wayside simply because they lack vision. They don't have any direction so they are stumbling through life, bouncing from one problem to the next like a pinball. You can't allow circumstances to dictate your direction like that.

Find the purpose God has for you. Seek the Lord and learn to hear His voice. Then set a goal and do something constructive with your life. Live your life so that when you are gone, people are going to miss you. You will have to leave the safety and security the world offers and take some chances, but that's why God sent the Holy Spirit to help you. Fruit grows out on the limb; you can't be a trunk-hugger and bear fruit. You have to get out on the limb, where you're blowing in the wind and hanging on for dear life.

Glorify God and recognize what He has done in your life. Remember that if worse comes to worst, you are going to heaven for all eternity. Be thankful and magnify God above your circumstances. Take control and begin to conceive the purposes of God in your imagination. Let the plan God has for you take root in your heart, see yourself fulfilling it, and then watch as it comes to pass.

Putting Your Imagination to Work

You won't fulfill God's plan for your life overnight. You have to be patient. It may take God some time to get you back on track and heading in the right direction, but if you make seeking God your lifestyle, things will start to happen. In a short period of time, your imagination will come alive. Your heart won't be darkened anymore. Instead, you will begin to hear and see things that you couldn't hear or see before. God will start directing you, putting you on track to fulfill His purpose for your life.

Father, I pray that the truths in this book have helped people to find, follow, and ultimately fulfill Your perfect will for their lives. Bring back to their remembrance the things You have spoken to them through these teachings and give them the wisdom to apply their lives to them. Thank you Jesus for the awesome things that are in store for each one of them. Amen!

Receive Jesus as Your Savior

Choosing to receive Jesus Christ as your Lord and Savior is the most important decision you'll ever make!

God's Word promises, "That if thou shalt confess with thy mouth the Lord Jesus, and shalt believe in thine heart that God hath raised him from the dead, thou shalt be saved. For with the heart man believeth unto righteousness; and with the mouth confession is made unto salvation" (Romans 10:9,10). "For whosoever shall call upon the name of the Lord shall be saved" (Romans 10:13).

By His grace, God has already done everything to provide salvation. Your part is simply to believe and receive.

Pray out loud: *Jesus, I confess that You are my Lord and Savior. I believe in my heart that God raised You from the dead. By faith in Your Word, I receive salvation now. Thank You for saving me.*

The very moment you commit your life to Jesus Christ, the truth of His Word instantly comes to pass in your spirit. Now that you're born again, there's a brand-new you.

Receive the Holy Spirit

As His child, your loving heavenly Father wants to give you the supernatural power you need to live a new life.

> *For every one that asketh receiveth; and he that seeketh findeth; and to him that knocketh it shall be opened...how much more shall your heavenly Father give the Holy Spirit to them that ask him?*

> *Luke 11:10-13*

All you have to do is ask, believe, and receive!

Pray: *Father, I recognize my need for Your power to live a new life. Please fill me with Your Holy Spirit. By faith, I receive it right now. Thank You for baptizing me. Holy Spirit, You are welcome in my life.*

Congratulations—now you're filled with God's supernatural power.

Some syllables from a language you don't recognize will rise up from your heart to your mouth. (1 Corinthians 14:14.) As you speak them out loud by faith, you're releasing God's power from within and building yourself up in the spirit. (1 Corinthians 14:4.) You can do this whenever and wherever you like.

It doesn't really matter whether you felt anything or not when you prayed to receive the Lord and His Spirit. If you believed in your heart that you received, then God's Word promises you did.

"Therefore I say unto you, What things soever ye desire, when ye pray, believe that ye receive them, and ye shall have them" (Mark 11:24). God always honors His Word—believe it!

Please contact me and let me know that you've prayed to receive Jesus as your Savior or to be filled with the Holy Spirit. I would like to rejoice with you and help you understand more fully what has taken place in your life. I'll send you a free gift that will help you understand and grow in your new relationship with the Lord. Welcome to your new life!

About the Author

Andrew's life was forever changed the moment he encountered the supernatural love of God on March 23, 1968. The author of more than thirty books, Andrew has made it his mission for more than five decades to change the way the world sees God.

Andrew's vision is to go as far and deep with the Gospel as possible. His message goes *far* through the *Gospel Truth* television and radio program, which is available to nearly half the world's population. The message goes *deep* through discipleship at Charis Bible College, founded in 1994, which currently has more than seventy campuses and over 6,000 students around the globe. These students will carry on the same mission of changing the way the world sees God. This is Andrew's legacy.

To contact Andrew Wommack please write, e-mail, or call:

Andrew Wommack Ministries, Inc.
P.O. Box 3333 • Colorado Springs, CO 80934-3333
E-mail: info@awmi.net
Helpline Phone (orders and prayer): 719-635-1111
Hours: 4:00 AM to 9:30 PM MST

Andrew Wommack Ministries of Europe
P.O. Box 4392 • WS1 9AR Walsall • England
E-mail: enquiries@awme.net
U.K. Helpline Phone (orders and prayer):
011-44-192-247-3300
Hours: 5:30 AM to 4:00 PM GMT

Or visit him on the Web at: **www.awmi.net**

YOU HAVE A DESTINY!
FIND IT AT CHARIS.

Teaching that combines the rich Word of God
with practical ministry experience

Nearly **60 campuses** across
the U.S. and around the world with
convenient **distance-education** options!

CHANGE
YOUR **LIFE**

CHANGE
THE **WORLD**

Visit **CharisBibleCollege.org**
or call **844-360-9577** for
all our program options

CHARIS®
BIBLE COLLEGE